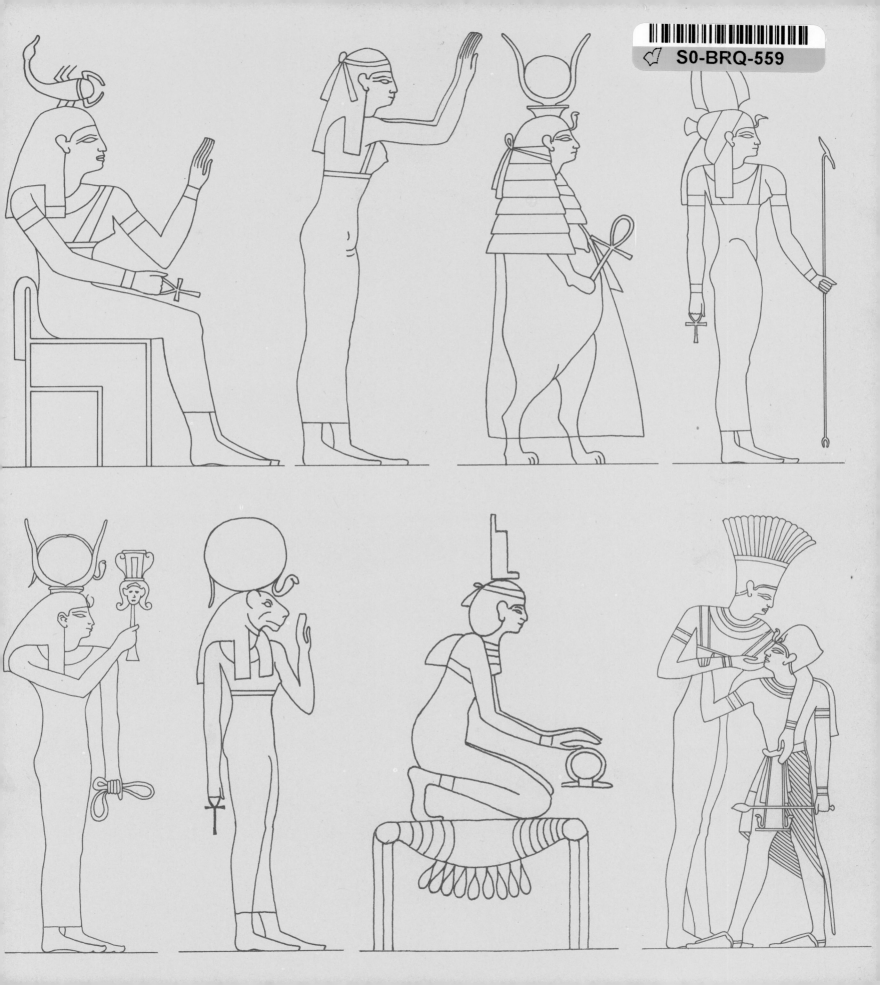

THE WOMAN IN EGYPTIAN ART

THE IMAGE OF WOMAN

STEFFEN WENIG

THE WOMAN IN EGYPTIAN ART

McGRAW-HILL Book Company
NEW YORK

Translated from the German by B. Fischer, Zurich

© The Hamlyn Publishing Group Ltd., 1969
Library of Congress Catalog Card No. 70-87839
McGraw-Hill Code No. 69280
Printed in the German Democratic Republic

Contents

TO MY WIFE

During ancient times the unique and enchanting country of Egypt drew foreigners into its spell. The customs of the Egyptians, their art and culture, aroused, above all, the interest and travelling urge of the ancient writers and scholars. Today the past of this country attracts modern man in a more unique way than all other civilizations of the ancient Orient. It is not only the mystery, monumentality or even splendour, but primarily the clear artistic expressiveness and constructive manner of representation characterized by its lack of perspectives that agrees with the artistic taste of our rationally disposed contemporaries.

As a result of this far-reaching and still growing interest many popular books dealing with Ancient Egypt are written every year throughout the world. If the publishers and author have decided to enlarge the wide range by yet another opus of this sort, it is with the intention of introducing to the reader a special subject about which relatively little literature has been available until now: Woman in Ancient Egypt.

The attempt has been made to depict a concise yet comprehensive image of woman's position in public and private life and of her possibilities and limitations. Although principally concerned with the Pharaonic period it is necessary to make references to the Ptolemaic and Roman periods to comment upon certain questions. The special literature which has been used and listed in the appendix reflects the present state of research and is meant to facilitate further investigation by any who wish to study specific problems more thoroughly.

Naturally only a selection of the abundant material can be presented here. A relatively large space has been reserved for written evidence because, thanks to the direct expressive power of words, the reader is familiarized with the Egyptian's language, which sometimes is prosaic and sometimes illustrative. Instead of writing a special chapter about woman in Egyptian art, the comments to the plates have been given in a more detailed manner.

The illustrations are meant to offer the reader a general view of the representations of woman during the different periods of Egyptian history from Prehistoric to Christian times. Without the amiable help of colleagues and friends to whom I am indebted for the photographs, it would not have been possible to have among these works of art examples which have rarely or never at all been shown before.

I would like to express my sincere gratitude to Chr. Desroches-Noblecourt (Louvre, Paris) and M. Matthieu† (Hermitage, Leningrad) as well as to B. V. Bothmer (The Brooklyn Museum, Brooklyn), I. E. S. Edwards (The British Museum, London), H. G. Fischer (The Metropolitan Museum of Art, New York), A. Greifenhagen and W. Kaiser (Staatliche Museen, Berlin-Charlottenburg), A. Klasens (Rijksmuseum van Oudheden, Leiden), H. W. Müller (Ägyptische Staatssammlung, Munich), W. Müller (Staatliche Museen, Berlin), E. Otto (Ägyptologisches Institut, Heidelberg), W. S. Smith† (Museum of Fine Arts, Boston), J. Vandier (Louvre, Paris) and to the directors of the following collections: Frühchristlich-byzantinische Abteilung and Münzkabinett der Staatlichen Museen, Berlin; Übersee-Museum, Bremen; Gulbenkian Museum of Oriental Art, Durham; Museo Archeologico, Florence; Egyptian Museum, Cairo; University College, London; State Pushkin Museum of Fine Arts, Moscow; Ashmolean

Museum, Oxford; Ikonen-Museum, Recklinghausen; The Virginia Museum of Fine Arts, Richmond; Egyptian Museum, Turin.

W. Forman, Prague, W. Sameh, Cairo and the Hirmer Verlag, Munich have helped with a series of colour and black-and-white photographs.

I. Becher and R. Tanner, Leipzig, granted me insight into their unpublished manuscripts; I am obliged to B. V. Bothmer, Brooklyn, and K. Parlasca, Frankfort on the Main for several references. I thank all of them most cordially, especially so S. Morenz, Leipzig, who not only gave me the permission to use the dissertations of Chr. Müller-Kriesel and R. Unger, which were written in his institute and have not yet been published, but also contributed a series of valuable suggestions and comments to the manuscript.

In a scenery characterized by contrasts – the fertile valley of the Nile and the barren desert – men of Pharaonic, Greek, and Roman times (cir. 3000 BC to AD 300) continuously erected new temples in honour of their gods and sovereigns and built an endless succession of tombs. They wished to rest there after death, which they did not believe to be an ending, but only a transition into a different form of existence. They also built cities whose splendour and fame shone forth throughout the Orient. But most things concerned with real life have vanished today. What remains is but a part of the many temples and the tombs destined for eternity, to serve man in the Afterworld.

No people on earth believed so consistently in a continuation of life in the Afterworld as did the Egyptians. The endeavours of each Egyptian were mainly directed towards two goals: to comport himself according to Ma'at, that is, order, justice and correctness, and to provide for the continuation of life in that Afterworld in good time. The tomb in which the mummified corpse rested was known as a "house of eternity." It was provided with whatever seemed indispensable for a living person. Originally, only the tomb equipment and offerings of food and drink were supplied for the deceased. But when monumental architecture was developed in the Third Dynasty (with the sepulchre of King Djoser), something was added. From now on the mastabas, sepulchral monuments characterized by a rectangular superstructure and sloping walls, had an offering chamber wherein one could display the deceased's nourishment and perform the religious rites. This chamber replaced the former modest offering recess. Everything else was reproduced by the representations on the walls, first by painted reliefs, later by wall-paintings, especially in the rock tombs. To begin with, the motifs referred to the death of the person in question: a proper funeral, the obsequies, and the constantly repeated offerings, which are shown as they are being prepared. Also secular scenes appear and increase in quantity throughout the Old Kingdom. Words and pictures often describe in an almost epic-like manner the dead person's private life, his offices and successes, his family – wife, children or parents – and his pleasures, his tasks and duties. This is combined with a portrayal of the labour performed on his estates. There we see the servants or the workmen and farmers of the feudal lord who, by their activity, assure the constant maintenance of the estate. These representations show what was necessary for the living as well as for the dead. For not only did the Egyptian believe firmly in a continuation of life beyond death, but he was also persuaded of the magical power of words. By means of ritual texts and the ceremony of the "Opening of the Mouth" the mortuary priests enlivened the images, which then began to act for the person buried in the tomb. For this reason he had himself surrounded by these scenes which were meant to assure him of an everlasting, good burial and continually provided him with the things he loved and cherished during his lifetime.

Thus it was not a desire for decoration that caused Egyptians to adorn their tombs with brightly coloured representations – originally they were only accessible to few people – but a necessity resulting from conceptions created by religious belief. Therefore, with some rare exceptions, true "art" does not exist in Egypt; the statues, reliefs and paintings were not made for a spectator, but only to be present and effective; thus, the aesthetic aspect falls away. Neither did the Egyptians have a word expressing "art." Their "artists" were artisans. The sculptor, for instance, who created the funerary portrait statues – the lasting body to replace the one of the disembodied dead person – was called "he who causes to be alive." In Egypt we encounter the same phenomenon that existed among other early civilizations and also as during the Middle Ages: art cannot be separated from religion and serves to realize religious conceptions.

If mainly from the New Kingdom on, the tombs assume monumental characteristics, the old basic significance is not altered. Certainly, some works are created for decorative reasons alone or nearly alone, but they remain individual cases. Looking at it from the Egyptian point of view, they must be considered as aberrations, a deviation from Ma'at.

Thanks to the mortuary belief of this people we are relatively well informed about its history, customs, and way of living. The long sequences of representations on the walls of the tombs not only give us the particulars of the buried person's individuality, but also of the social conditions of the working people, of the state and of the development of handicraft and agriculture.

Coffin inscriptions or long papyrus scrolls containing religious texts, which were put into the deceased's tomb from the time of the New Kingdom, as well as the monumental inscriptions and representations on the walls of the tem-

ples built for gods and kings, give an idea of the Egyptians' religious world.

But we also obtain our knowledge about Ancient Egypt from other sources, such as statues and tombstones with biographical texts; official documents – royal decrees which were written on stelae and erected in the temple; papyri and potsherds made of limestone or clay, containing administrative texts from the temple archives; records; settlements of accounts, contracts, and receipts, as well as inscriptions left on the monuments and the faces of cliffs by visitors; and literary texts and instructions, stories, and tales or love poems. These grant us the best insight into the pleasures of daily life as well as its worries and difficulties.

Relatively little of the actual dwelling places of the Egyptians has remained for us to see, because the limited space in the valley of the Nile forced them to constantly build upon the ruins of the past. One exception is Akhenaten's city, Tell el Amarna, which was not repopulated after the king's death and has been preserved for us underneath the protecting sands of the centuries as a complete community, showing the remains of its palaces, temples and dwelling houses.

These sources which are capable of giving various kinds of evidence recreate Ancient Egypt and its people for us. They are the object of the Egyptologists' work as they gather mosaic stone beside mosaic stone, either as philologists, historians, or archaeologists, to obtain a uniform and comprehensive image and contribute in this manner to the discovery of the history of mankind.

The Social
and Legal Situation
of Woman

Contrary to the women of most ancient civilizations, Rome and Greece included, the Egyptian woman enjoyed the same rights as man, not only de jure but also de facto. For oriental circumstances this is most unusual, and it is reflected by inscriptions, records, and works of art. Probably the reason for this must be seen in the fact that Egyptian society as a whole was represented by a divine king. Thus man and woman were not seen in their familiar relationship but rather with regard to the royal political centre of society and, in this relationship, as sharing equal rights (37).*

It is hardly necessary to mention that the legal situation was based upon the difference between the social ranks, as is the case among all class societies, and therefore never could be uniform. When we speak subsequently of equal rights accorded to both, men and women, these always concern members of the same class.

The sources at our disposal and from which we shall quote, show that woman was always highly esteemed. Not only was she represented at her husband's or son's side in the tombs, but at times more emphasis was put on the maternal than on the paternal parentage. Only the Ptolemaic Period brought about changes, as foreign, i.e., Greek, conceptions and conditions slowly began to influence and supplant Egyptian law. Nevertheless, both systems of law existed side by side for a long time and Egyptians as well as foreigners could decide freely whether they wanted to base their settlements upon Greek or Egyptian law. The binding element for the contracting parties was the language in which the settlement was made.

So far no Pharaonic law book has been found, such as the codex of the Babylonian king Hammurabi of the eighteenth century BC, in which the rights and duties of each person were fixed; nevertheless, such a work must have existed. Not only do we find references to general laws in legal texts – "Pharaoh speaketh" – but we also possess an unpublished papyrus of the third century BC from Hermopolis, and law notes of the Ptolemaic Period. So far we can only examine and evaluate the preserved monuments, es-

* Numbers in brackets refer to the Bibliography p. 57.

pecially those containing legal matters, with regard to the questions which interest us.

It is possible to trace back the social equality of rights between men and women to Prehistoric times. Excavations of cemeteries have revealed that like men, women could possess their own tombs with the adequate equipment, and later on their own statues and tombstones as well. It is significant that the equality of rights even existed in the sphere of mortuary belief, thus disclosing this principle as a part of human existence. The fact that the many tombs of women belonging to the various social classes – queens, princesses, ladies of honour, wives of functionaries and of workers – do not differ from those of their men with regard to their equipment demonstrates this throughout all the historical periods of Pharaonic Egypt.

The first direct evidence which can give an answer to our questions dates from the Old and Middle Kingdom. Although the bulk of the papyrus manuscripts containing records and contracts has come down to us chiefly from the Late and the Ptolemaic Periods, they have a certain validity for the earlier periods.

During the period we have outlined, woman's full competence relating to law and business – an essential characteristic of equal rights – extended to all legally defined areas. A woman could dispose of private property, such as land, servants, and slaves, money or materials, and administrate it according to her own free and independent will. She could conclude any kind of settlement, appear as contracting partner in marriage contracts, execute testaments, free slaves, make adoptions, or officiate as a witness of records. Finally, she was even entitled to sue at law, and it can hardly be doubted that the maidservant received the same payment in natural products as the manservant. For example, there are representations dating from the Old Kingdom which show how female weavers were rewarded.

Contrary to Greek law, the Egyptian woman did not need a guardian to be able to execute legal acts, neither did it matter whether she was married or not.

She had several possibilities of acquiring personal wealth.

The most frequent were inheritances from her parents; furthermore, a woman could acquire property through gifts from her parents or husband, or through purchases. In general, one concluded contracts at devolutions of property, that is, when donations or purchases were made. A biographical inscription from the Old Kingdom relates that a man received 50 arouras (about 13.5 hectares) of arable land from his mother. Thanks to a stele of a later period, now in Berlin, we know that when the office of a mortuary priest passed on from father to daughter by inheritance, the right to dispose of his property was included: "as far as all these people who were bequeathed to me by my father, are concerned, I do not allow anyone to have authority over them." This is followed by the enumeration by name of the servants. A different case reports that a widow had to care for the equipment of her husband's tomb and received his entire property in return. According to the general legal conditions, a wife was entitled to a third of her husband's possessions after his death, whereas the other two-thirds had to be divided among the children and sisters and brothers of the testator.

If one wished to avoid this condition, for instance, to enable the wife to receive either a larger part of the estate or the right to dispose of the entire fortune, the husband had to undertake certain steps. Thus one could transmit property by means of donations. In a settlement of the late Middle Kingdom a man left 15 captives to his wife and children. At the same time 60 other captives are mentioned, which the wife had received from her husband at an earlier occasion.

In a different text it is said:

"Date. Bestowal record of X. I formulate a bestowal record in favour of my wife ... Sopdu's daughter Satshefet, called Teti, concerning all things which my brother ... Y transmitted to me together with the implements belonging to it, concerning everything that he has transmitted to me. She shall bequeath it as she pleases to one of the children that she will have born to me. Furthermore, I bequeath to her the three Asians which my brother has transmitted to me, and she shall bequeath them to whichever of her children she pleases. Concerning my tomb, I wish to be buried in it with my wife and do not permit it to be used illegally by anyone else. Furthermore, as to the chambers that my brother ... Y built for me, my wife shall live in them and I do not permit her to be expelled by anyone. (In the case of my death) Z. shall be the tutor of my son" (after Wolf, 72).

Adoption represented another possibility of devolving property. In a famous document of adoption dating from the Twentieth Dynasty the critical passage reads:

"On this day ... Nebnufer, my husband, made a writing for me, the musician of Setekh Nenufer, and made me a child of his, and wrote down unto me all he possessed, having no son or daughter apart from myself. All profit that I have made with her, I will bequeath it to Nenufer, my wife, lest (any of) my own brothers or sisters arise to confront her at my death tomorrow or thereafter and say 'Let my brother's share be given (to me)' ..." (after Gardiner, 21).

The purpose of this adoption is crystal clear. The object was to prevent the husband's sisters and brothers from demanding their share of his property upon his death, since he had intended it to be entirely for his wife. The same papyrus also describes (see p. 22) how the woman shelters and brings up the three children of the female slave they had acquired together. After her husband's death she marries the eldest of the two girls to her younger brother, whom she then adopts, so that he may receive the same share of the inheritance.

Thus we can see that a woman was absolutely free to dispose of her own property, which sometimes was separated from that of her husband during their married life. Under these circumstances the remarkable situation can occur in which the wife lends her husband money for three years at a rate of interest of 30 percent, which he must warrant with his own goods.

Neither are we astonished to learn that she could dispose freely of her inheritance and exclude the children from it if she wanted to. Naunakhte, a woman who lived during the New Kingdom, made use of this possibility in her testament. Before a local tribunal consisting of 14 persons, of which only two were foreign district officers, while the others acted as jurors, Naunakhte introduces herself as a free woman and determines that not all of her eight children from her second marriage shall inherit. "But see, I am grown old, and see, they (the children) are not looking after me in my turn. Whoever of them has aided me, to him I will give of my property." Then the children are listed by name with the account of who shall inherit fully, who only partly and who not at all. The latter are introduced by the phrase: "List of her children of whom she said: 'They shall not participate in the division of my one-third, but in the two-thirds of their father they shall participate'" (after Černy, 12).

If, however, no settlement of donation or adoption exists, the remaining two-thirds are automatically transferred to the children without the wife's being able to raise a protest. Apart from these examples, there are many other kinds of contracts which were concluded by women. Their number constantly increases towards the Ptolemaic Period. What made the settlement of contracts valid was a list of the names of witnesses present. Thus, contracts which did not specify the identity of witnesses were considered to be merely drafts. The range of possible contracts is very large. It includes marriage settlements, with which we shall deal further on; agreements concerning horticulture; engagements of wet nurses and even arrangements about self-enslavement. Although this self-enslavement was forbidden, it repeatedly occurred. One tried to avoid this law by formulating a clause which limited the self-enslavement to a period of "99 years." Diverse reasons could lead a person to such an action. In a Late-Ptolemaic settlement dating from the years 42/41 BC, which is supposed to be a translation from Demotic into Greek, it is arranged that a woman who owes money sells herself to her creditor and binds herself to do whatever is demanded of her, day and night. In return, the creditor must provide for her in every way (1). The desire to be assured of one's provision could lead a person as far as selling oneself to a temple and even paying a monthly fee. This amount must have been identical with the monthly salary the woman received from the temple. The following document of a self-enslavement dates from the thirty-third year of the reign of Ptolemy Euergetes II:

"Hath said the female servant NN ... before my master Soknebtynis, the great god: 'I am thy servant together with my children and my children's children; I shall not be able to be free in thy precincts for ever and ever. Thou shalt protect me, thou shalt keep me safe, thou shalt guard me, thou shalt keep me sound, thou shalt protect me from every demon, ... etc.

I will give thee 1¼ kite in copper ... (for) my rent of service in each month ... till the completion of 99 years, and I will give it to thy priests monthly'..." (after Thompson, 65).

This case of self-enslavement, which indeed is not a very unusual one, shows that one must apply a different standard to slavery in Egypt than in Greece or Rome. In Egypt it only gained a certain importance from the New Kingdom on (see also p. 16).

If a woman believed that someone had wronged her, she naturally had the same right as a man to seek justice by legal process before a regular tribunal. A private dispute which, since it was of no general importance, was handled by a local tribunal of Western Thebes, has been summed up on a limestone ostracon as follows:

"On this day. Accusation made by the citizen Isis against the workmen Khaemopet, Khaemweset and Amenakht: 'The sites of my husband, Penakht, shall be given to me.' One took counsel with each other. The judicial sentence: 'She is right. One shall give the sites of her husband to her' ..." (after Lüddeckens, 33).

Further examples of this kind can be found up to the Ptolemaic Period (29).

Up to now we have been analyzing the equality of rights from the legal point of view; but how was the situation in other respects? To name but a few examples, did a woman have the same possibility as a man of being educated – did she have a "right to education," as we would say nowadays? Could she also hold public offices? These and similar questions cannot be answered in a general manner, for we must always consider the respective social rank of the woman, which was decisive. Naturally, the members of the upper classes had an entirely different situation than the women among the labourers, peasants or artisans, not to mention serfs and slaves. Most of the middle class women also had to work to earn their living. They often had land at their disposal – either as property or on lease – which surely cannot have been very extensive and probably just provided for their own livelihood. If this was not the case, then husband and wife took a position on the estates of the rich, the royal palace, or the temple, where they worked in the fields, in the workshops, or in the house. There they lived under patriarchal circumstances and, as servants, they were entrusted with special tasks. At harvest the women mainly took over the job of winnowing and sifting the corn. Other occupations consisted of taking care of the household, grinding the grain (Plate 17b), kneading the dough for making bread and working as weavers and spinners (Ill. p. 15). Some of them knew how to write, as personal signatures of witnesses on Late Period documents show. But they were hardly numerous. Generally only people belonging to the class of scribes could learn how to write, since this usually involved a special education. Nevertheless, other classes also had people capable of writing, among whom there may have been many a woman. Our sources only give us little information concerning these questions, but one can assume that at least queens and princesses knew how to write. A representation of a princess holding writing materials dating from the Old Kingdom gives evidence of this. By chance the teacher of Hatshepsut's daughter, Nefrure, is known to us. He was the queen's favourite and the architect of the terraced temple of Deir el Bahri, Sennemut. We also know of a woman scribe who belonged to the household of a queen of the Thirteenth Dynasty. But since in professional life man had precedence over woman, it seldom was necessary for her to learn the complicated system of writing.

Eloquence was the essential and most sought after cultural value. It was even valued higher than the knowledge of writing. A passage from the Instruction of Ptahhotep reads: "Eloquence is more hidden than the emerald, yet it may be found with maidservants at the grindstone" (after Erman, 19).

Woman seldom appeared in public life. In general her work was limited to the home and family. This is not a case

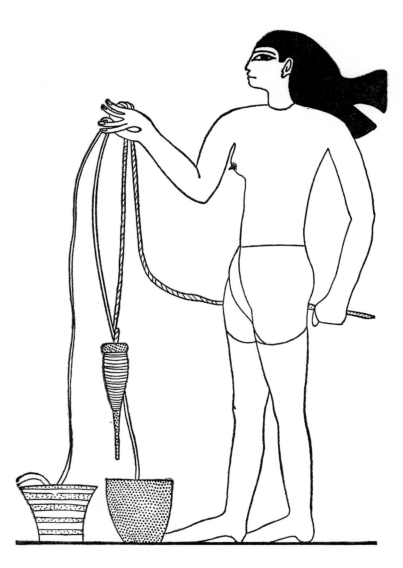

of inferior legal rights but a consequence of the part played by the son, who, as executor of the mortuary offerings, holds the primary position in public life. Nevertheless, some women did hold public offices. We encounter, for instance, a manageress of the dining hall and headmistress of the wig workshop; others are headmistresses of the singers, of the amusements or of the house of weavers, mistresses of the royal harem or superintendents of houses. If during the later periods the wives of eminent persons or members of old noble families procured high official titles for themselves, we can assume that they were purely honorary.

Except for members of the lowest social classes, women also had the possibility of serving in the temple of a divinity. It seems, that from the New Kingdom on, women could be admitted to temple service without regard to their social position. The priestesses we know from this epoch, mainly from Thebes – where certainly many held the office for honour's sake alone – are recruited not only from members of the royal house, the civil service, or clergy, but also from the working class. Offices of this sort were inheritable like all others so that their bearers could dispose of them freely. We know that Queen Ahmose Nefertari passed on the office of a Second Priest in the temple of Amon in Karnak to her brother for a payment.

A woman performing the duties of an office in the temple of a divinity or in the royal cult was mainly limited to being a musician, either as a singer or as an instrumentalist. Therefore she was required to be skilled in these arts, in which she generally became proficient as a young girl.

We find women as priestesses of the lowest rank, mainly in temples of goddesses, such as Hathor or Neith. But they could also have posts in the sanctuaries of the gods, and, finally, during the Ptolemaic Period every temple had a certain number of sistrum players or singers. Like the male members of the temple they were divided into groups called 'phylai.' Their leaders, called "big ones of the musicians" were mostly wives of high functionaries (in Egypt celibacy never existed). Occasionally, we also encounter high priestesses, in particular of Hathor and Satet, who were appointed by the king. Perhaps these also were merely honorary offices but nevertheless they involved remarkable incomes. As a rule, higher positions than that of a mistress of a phyle, or a temple treasurer were not attainable, with the exception of the Divine Consorts in the periods following the New Kingdom. Apart from these occupations, women were engaged as dancers in the cult, or as professional actresses who portrayed the two female mourners, Isis and Nephtys, in the mysteries or during the funeral rites. Finally woman could be engaged as mortuary priestess on the temple domains – we have already had one example above – where she had to look after the preparations of the offerings intended for the deceased. She lived on the revenues of this property, which were not permitted to be used elsewhere. If in one case we encounter a woman-judge, it must be considered an exception.

It is interesting to learn about the rights and possibilities of foreign women in Egypt.

At all times foreigners came into the country. As far as their cultural development was concerned, the neighbours in the south had remained behind Egypt so that a strong impulse to settle in the cities and villages along the Nile and to earn one's living there always prevailed.

However, most foreign women came to Egypt involuntarily as prisoners and arrived on the estates of feudal lords or temple institutions as bondmaids or slaves. There they lived together with the Egyptians in a patriarchal manner, especially during the earlier periods. But military expeditions, and therefore also the acquisition of prisoners, were so seldom that the few slaves were of no economic importance at all. Of course, there was a change later on when the monarchs of the New Kingdom strove for conquests in grand style and as a result many people were brought into the country as cheap labour. Not all of these women were destined for low class services. If they were beautiful enough, they could be admitted into the harem or be engaged as musicians or dancers. As several examples show, they were often given their freedom.

From the New Kingdom on, there were so many foreigners of all classes in Egypt that there was nothing extraordinary about them and they could hold the highest offices. If they were free, they had the same rights as the Egyptians, and foreign slaves could hardly be distinguished from their Egyptian equals.

Love, Marriage and Motherhood

The evidences, which have survived the years, give us a fairly good insight into the many aspects of the Egyptians' life. Yet the most intimate sphere of human relationship – love between two people – has always been treated with the greatest reserve. Only occasionally does the Egyptian refer to this in word or picture.

Thus, for example, we never hear what made a man consummate a marriage. Could a young man marry the girl of his choice, or did his parents select his future wife, a custom still quite prevalent in the Near East today? Judging by the sources, pure love marriages must have been rare. In a biographical inscription we read about a woman who lived at the time of Ptolemy XI: "My father gave me to NN as a wife." We surely are not wrong when we assume that economic and social factors were important considerations in the marriage arrangements and should not be underestimated.

The representations of married couples in the tombs are the few examples of tender harmony that we know from the Old and Middle Kingdoms. Either the spouses hold each other by their hands (Plate 11), or the wife puts her arm around the waist of her husband (Plate 5). This gesture alone expresses the consorts' sincere relationship. In portraits it is even rarer that the husband embraces his wife. The particularly extensive literature, which has been handed down to us from the Middle Kingdom, limits its descriptions to domestic happiness and praise of the wife, whereas one is warned of familiar acquaintance with frivolous girls or with the wives of friends and colleagues:

"If thou desirest to make friendship last in a home to which thou hast access as master, as a brother, or as a friend, into any place where thou mightest enter, beware of approaching the women. It does not go well with the place where that is done. The face has no alertness by splitting it (perhaps: He who has a wandering eye for the women cannot be keen). A thousand men may be distracted from their (own) advantage. A mere trifle, the likeness of a dream – and one attains death through knowing her ..." (from the Instruction of Ptahhotep, after Wolf, 72). The same tenor is expressed in the Instruction of Anii from the New Kingdom, where the following advice is given:

"Be on thy guard against a woman from abroad, who is not known in her (own) town. Do not stare at her when she passes by. Do not know her carnally ..." (after Erman, 19).

Only once, in a fairy tale, do we hear of a love affair between a married woman and a "citizen." We shall come back to this subject later on.

Nevertheless, the Egyptian was not averse to sensual pleasures. As a result of the disorders that shook the foundations of the Egyptian view of the world between the Old and Middle Kingdoms, there arose a general scepticism, which soon developed into a strong desire for enjoying life more intensely. The Harpist's Songs, which were still very popular during the New Kingdom, praise the present moment:

"Be happy ... follow thy desire as long as thou shalt live. Put myrrh upon thy head and clothing of fine linen upon thee, being anointed with genuine marvels of the god's property" for "there is none who comes back from (over) there that he may tell their state ..." (after Erman, 19).

A remarkable change took place during the New Kingdom. Works of art and literature show to a much greater extent than before the personal relationship between two people. The changed intellectual disposition of this period becomes apparent when, for example, King Amenophis III celebrates on commemorative scarabs his wedding to his wife Tiy, who was of common origin and consequently not worthy of his rank. In a way similar to our use of badges today, these scarabs recorded a certain event and were distributed among the courtiers. In the eleventh year of his reign, this same king had a pleasure lake laid out for his consort.

> "His Majesty gave orders for a lake to be laid out
> for the sublime Queen Tiy – may she live –
> on her property: 'Pastime of the evening'
> being 3,700 cubits long and 700 cubits wide"
>
> (after Schott, 50).

The sincere relationship between the two is also visible elsewhere. Thus, years after her husband's death, Tiy had a little wooden tablet made which shows the couple in a loving embrace. It is of no consequence – at least not in oriental circumstances – that this very pharaoh possessed a tremendous harem (see pp. 37/38).

Likewise, the relationship between Amenophis IV/Akhenaten and his wife Nefertiti was very cordial, at least during the first years of their marriage. This can be seen on many representations. Yet it must be regarded as an absolute exception that scenes of strictly private character were depicted, such as the king kissing his daughter, whom he holds on his lap, Nefertiti nursing one of the children, a princess eating a duck (Plate 64), and other scenes of this type. This exhibition of family life can be explained by the religious and artistic reform prompted by this pharaoh. It also expresses political tendencies which cannot be discussed here. Likewise, the stele in Berlin entitled the "Promenade in the Garden," which depicts the young royal couple – perhaps Tutankhaten (who later calls himself Tutankhamon) and Ankhesenpa-aten (later Ankhesenamen), belongs to the art of the Amarna Period (Plate 67). The queen holds out a bouquet of flowers for her husband to smell. The Egyptians, who were very indebted to tradition and used to seeing their pharaoh as a sublime, divine person, must have been shocked by the representation of such intimate and human scenes. This was one of the reasons why the reforming efforts of Akhenaten were abandoned to persecution and oblivion after his death.

The documents of private persons also show the sincere harmony of married couples and young lovers. Most extraordinary is the letter of a widower to his deceased wife Ankhiri, in which he asks her what evil he had done her, since he now is in a "wretched state." He justifies himself with eloquent words but doesn't forget to threaten that he will accuse her in front of the tribunal of the gods of the West:

"What have I done to thee? I made thee a married woman when I was a youth ... I was with thee, and did not put thee away. I did not cause thy heart to grieve ... And everything which came to me before thee, did I not receive it on thy account saying 'I will act according to thy desire?' ... I hid nothing from thee in thy day of life. I did not cause thee to suffer pain in aught that I did with thee, after the fashion of a lord. Nor did'st thou find me (?) disregarding (?) thee after the fashion of a peasant in entering into a strange house ..." (after Schott, 50). Then the man describes how he provided for her and called for the master physician to treat her when she was ill. Finally he assures her of not having remarried for three years after her death on account of her.

In a letter which a scribe sends to a far-off friend, he sends greetings from his sweetheart who stayed at home: "The singer of Amon, Isetnofret says: 'How art thee? How much I long to see thee. My eyes are as big as Memphis because I hunger to see thee. And I say here to Thot and all gods of the house of Thot: may thou be in health! May thou live! May thou be praised for whatever thou doest!'" (after Schott, 50). The tender tone of this greeting reminds us of the love songs which are mostly preserved for us on limestone ostraca and in three big papyri manuscripts of the Nineteenth and Twentieth Dynasties. They appeared as a new form of literature during the Eighteenth Dynasty. Love poetry has several patterns and often employs the so-called herdsman or servant travesty (26). The attributes of the beloved person are praised in beautiful language and preferably compared with concepts of a fowler's life:

"The charm of the resting-place is bewildering
(the mouth) of my mistress is a flower-bud
her breasts are love-apples
her arms look like clasps
her brow is the willow-wood trap
and I am a wild goose.
My (eyes) take her hair for bait
in the trap that is ready to close" (after Schott, 50).

It is not astonishing that love poetry glorifying sensual love developed especially during the New Kingdom. Egypt had stepped out of its voluntary isolation and brought home rich loot consisting of raw materials and slaves from the big expeditions to Asia Minor and the Sudan. This endowed the country with a well-being hitherto unknown. At the same time, the Egyptians came into contact with foreign morals and customs, some of which made their way into the country on the Nile. Above all, Syria had an influence

Astarte on Horseback

upon Egyptian life. Syrian divinities, for instance, among whom the goddesses Kadesh and Astarte (Ill. p. 19) are the most prominent, were worshipped in Egypt. Musical instruments, such as the lyre and the lute, were also imported. The erotism, which becomes apparent in the love poems or in the dances performed at banquets, can also be traced back to Syria where a less constrained way of life prevailed. Of course this was welcomed by the Egyptians, who lived in a luxurious and splendid style.

This also explains the highly feminine character of this period which forms such a heavy contrast to the masculine attitude of mind of the past times (61; 72). Feminine gracefulness became the beauty ideal of the New Kingdom and influenced even the masculine portraits (30). Woman now stood at the centre of social life. On the whole, clothing, cosmetics and music obviously had become means of heightening the sensual faculties during this period. Transparent clothes did more to accentuate the charms of her body than to cover them. Dancers and maidservants – many probably from Syria – wore only a pubic belt (Plate 38) that increased the erotic effect. The present moment was celebrated and enjoyed. No important tomb of the Eighteenth Dynasty was without scenes of lavish banquets (Plates 37–41) where ample justice was done to the wine. It is typical of the Egyptian, who was always ready for fun and mockery, that he also depicted the after-effects of too much wine drinking (Ill. p. 20). During the Nineteenth and Twentieth Dynasties these images of gay festivities disappear, and from now on can only be part of the cult celebrations. This change of mental attitude goes so far that in a Theban tomb painting from the middle of the Eighteenth Dynasty, which was reused under Ramses II, the naked maidservants and girls were painted over with garments in the style of the Ramesside period (51). The reason for this sudden prudishness and reserve concerning the tomb paintings may have been a reaction against the decline in morality. Nevertheless, the pursuit of sensual pleasure did not cease. According to all we know, it must have even increased and been intensified by the use of various aphrodisiacs, about which a special book existed. Love magic had been used since the Middle

Kingdom, but then it was employed to heighten the sexual potency of the deceased in order to assure him descendants in the Hereafter. During the New Kingdom, however, it was destined for daily use.

A teacher repeatedly warns his pupils of sitting in the wine-taverns, of drinking too much beer or wine, and of having bad acquaintance with prostitutes. He then admonishes them to be diligent instead. This subject is illustrated in the so-called "Erotic Papyrus" from Turin, which describes the adventures of an inexperienced man in a brothel, and has remained unpublished on account of its extremely obscene representations. But erotic motives are not new in Egyptian art. One can indicate occasional representations of the *coitus per anum* during the Middle Kingdom and the rule of the Hyksos. Cases of adultery, rape, concubinage or polygamy were especially frequent in the artisan settlement of Western Thebes at the end of the New Kingdom. Here, of course, these phenomena are not the consequences of a life in which wealth has caused self-indulgent and intemperate behaviour. On the contrary, they reflect the rapidly increasing impoverishment of the lowest classes of the people, and the ensueing misery and moral instability. Disregarding exceptions of this sort, the Egyptians as a rule practised monogamy. This was also recorded by the Greek historian Herodotus (II, 92), who indeed contradicts Diodorus (I, 80), since the latter remarked that monogamy only applied to the priests, whereas any other man could have several wives. It is certain that polygamy was not against the law in Pharaonic Egypt. During the Old Kingdom it was limited to the royal house, but from the First Intermediate Period it was also common among private persons. Possibly the reason for the extension of this prerogative lies in the "democratization," which eventually allowed royal privileges to be transmitted to noblemen and commoners. As a rule, polygamy, i.e., the matrimonial alliance with more than one woman, and the institution of a harem – which originally was a privilege of the king and only passed on to nobility at a very late period – were automatically prevented by economic reasons and always remained limited to relatively few cases right into the Greco-Roman Period. Besides, lawful wedlock as a legal institution regulated the wife's security, the legitimation and provision of the children, and questions concerning the right of succession. Concubinage also existed, but we cannot say much about its form and expansion. The maidservants *eo ipso* belonged to the landlord who had engaged them, and adultery was not considered a sin when committed by a man. Apparently the children of such unions had no rights and could only be put on an equal level with the legitimate children through the act of adoption.

One knows little about the common age for getting married because, as we shall see, it was not indicated on the so-called marriage settlements. But mostly one married at the beginning of puberty, which meant for boys at the age of 15 and for girls at the age of 12 or 13 years. The woman mentioned on page 17 was 14 years old when her father gave her to be married.

Since the Egyptian had no notion of incest, he did not consider consanguinity as an impediment to marriage. We often encounter brother and sister couples in mythological stories – the most famous being Isis and Osiris – and the same appears in a fable of the Late Period. From this, one might conclude that marriage between brother and sister was more or less common in Egypt. Nevertheless, it is a fact that in private circles we only encounter it for certain during the Twenty-second Dynasty. An inquiry into the records of more than 490 marriages consummated during the Middle Kingdom showed that perhaps two can be taken as brother-and-sister marriages, whereas matrimonial alliances between half-brothers and sisters may have been more numerous (13). But in the royal house, brother-and-sister marriages occurred rather frequently indeed; it was even possible for the pharaoh to marry his own daughter, as is probably the case with Amenophis IV and Ramses II (7). Of course, we must give due consideration to the fact that it is most difficult to authenticate this type of marriage in Egypt, because from the reign of Tuthmosis III the mistress and wife is also called "sister" (13).

From the time of Ptolemy II on, it became a rule in the reigning family that the pharaoh marries his own sister. The Ptolemies may have taken over this custom from Greece (36).

From now on brother-and-sister marriages increase among private circles, too. While only one case is known from the Ptolemaic Period, they can be authenticated very frequently during the Roman Period. Although marriages between consanguine persons were strictly prohibited for Roman citizens, they remained allowed for aliens. An examination of 161 marriages showed that 38 were contracted between brothers and sisters (64). The reason for this increase in brother-and-sister marriages may be found in the agricultural structure of Egyptian economy, for only in that way could one successfully avoid the division of the landed property (36).

In general, one married within one's own social class, but of course there were also exceptions. Apparently, Egyptians could marry foreigners at all times. There are many examples of this from the royal house, where foreign women as a rule could only be concubines or ladies of the harem. Only Ramses II raised a princess from the land of the Hittites to the rank of the "Great Royal Consort" (see also p. 37). On a stele from Amarna, now in Berlin, a Syrian drinking beer is represented, whose Egyptian wife sits facing him. There usually was no impediment to a marriage between a free person and a slave. There are several interesting proofs of this. In a contract copied on a statuette is said:

"Year 27 under the rule of Tuthmosis (III). The royal barber Sabastet came before the tribunal (?) of the royal house to speak: 'My slave, my property, whom I acquired (myself), his name is Imenjui, I fetched him with my own strength, when I accompanied the sovereign. I gave him the daughter of my sister Nebta as a wife, her name is Takamenet . . .'" (after de Linage, 32).

It is not known, whether slaves were allowed to marry among themselves, but we certainly hear of no impediment in this respect.

In the above mentioned papyrus concerning adoption, it is explained that the woman Naunakhte and her husband bought a slave who gave life to three children – two girls and a boy. Certainly these were the children by her husband, who had passed away in the meantime. The woman, who had no children of her own, took them into her care and brought them up. Later on her younger brother married the elder of the two girls, who then was set free by the woman on the condition that her children shall also be free. At the same time she freed the other two adoptive children and adopted her brother, who was also her son-in-law, so that all four can inherit in the same degree (compare with p. 13).

It was the ideal of every man to marry young and have children. One wished to have boys rather than girls, because they could take over the father's office and carry out the offering service for the deceased parents as mortuary priests. "Take to thyself a wife while thou art (still) a youth that she may produce a son for thee. Beget (him) for thyself while thou art still young," it is said in an Instruction of the New Kingdom, that Ani made for his son's education (after Schott, 50). But: "Do not marry a godless wife, lest she brings up your children badly."

Whether an engagement period preceded the marriage is not mentioned anywhere. We know just as little about the formalities and festivities surrounding a marriage. Only the story of Prince Setna mentions the wedding of a royal brother and sister. Their father, the pharaoh, has the bride and a rich dowry brought into the bridegroom's house by night. On the following day a big celebration starts.

The Egyptian had several expressions for "getting married" – take a wife, found a household, enter a house. The young girl was, as already mentioned, given into marriage by the parents, after the young man had asked them for the hand of their daughter. Hereby the family ties were legally broken off. The father was the girl's legal substitute and after his death the mother could replace him. Two passages in the love poems indeed give cause for thought, since they clearly relate to the fact that the consent to the marriage depended on the mother: "He (the beloved one) knoweth not my desire to embrace him or he would send to my mother" (after Schott, 50).

After the marriage special designations were applied to the woman. Above all, she now held the title "mistress of the house," which signifies that she was responsible for the house, while the man, as superintendent of the household, pursued his professional activities.

One of the principles of conduct for a man towards a

woman was that he should treat her well during their married life. This is constantly postulated in the Instructions. Thus, in the Instruction of Ptahhotep, dating from the Old Kingdom, it is said:

"If thou art a man of standing, thou shouldst found thy household and love thy wife at home as is fitting. Fill her belly and clothe her back. Ointment is the prescription for her body. Make her heart glad, as long as thou livest. She is a profitable field for her lord" (after Wolf, 72).

In the Instruction of Anii the following advice is given:

"Thou shouldst not supervise (too closely) thy wife in her (own) house, when thou knowest that she is efficient. Do not say to her: 'Where is it? Fetch (it) for us!' when she has put (it) in the most useful place" (after Erman, 19).

Gallantry towards the ladies has not been described in the literature; but a relevant scene does exist in the tomb of Sechem-ka, who was an officer of justice during the Old Kingdom. There a man is represented who relieves a woman of a food basket which she carries on her head.

During the wedding or, at a later period, also after the marriage had been contracted, so-called marriage settlements were concluded. About a hundred examples dating from the periods after the New Kingdom have been handed down to us (33). Probably they were originally concluded between the bride's father and the husband; but later on the wife herself becomes a contracting partner, which – along with children who often already exist – indicates that the settlements were only made after the wedding. They demonstrate that the woman's rights were not diminished by her marriage. Furthermore, it is remarkable that the contracting partners mainly came from the middle class.

There existed two kinds of settlements; in one case the man had to make a payment at the wedding, the so-called "woman's portion," in the other – proved only from the sixth century BC on – the woman had to deliver a certain amount to the man. Most of the time they were composed according to fixed formulas of which several examples existed. In them the two contractors – the husband and the wife – and the parents of both were named, but without a personal description; we only know the husband's profession, and usually his origin. Many foreigners, such as Greeks, Nubians, or Blemmyes also concluded settlements based upon Egyptian law in this manner. Occasionally, they also mention a relative of the husband who had given his consent to the marriage. Furthermore, the notary or the scribe who had composed it is noted. On the reverse were written names of the witnesses. Their number oscillates (between 3 and 36) and never includes a woman during the Late Period. They could either sign for themselves – as was the custom until the end of the Late Period – or their names were listed by a scribe. The settlements were then kept by a third person or in the temple, where there must have been a register of these contracts. Marriage settlements are made up of clauses, of which a great number exists, but not all had to be included in the contract. Following the date and the names of the contracting parties are the marriage clauses; the clause concerning the woman's portion, that is, the amount which the husband had to give to the wife, perhaps originally evolved from the purchase-money; and the clause concerning the provision, by which the husband engages himself to guarantee the woman's provision during her married life. Usually a certain amount of money, corn, oil, and clothes, which varies individually, is agreed upon. Furthermore, there are the divorce clause as well as clauses concerning the children, the dowry – the personal property brought into the marriage by the woman – and, in conclusion, the form of oath by which the husband confirms his obligations towards the wife. Occasionally, the husband signs the contract himself, which is an additional assurance for the wife.

In the year 219 BC, under the rule of Ptolemy IV, the following settlement was composed (Papyrus Hauswaldt 6):

"The Blemmyan born in Egypt, Horemheb, son of X, his mother is Y, to the woman Tais, daughter of A, her mother is B: I have made thee a married woman (*marriage clause*). As thy portion I gave thee two pieces of silver, that is 15 staters (Greek currency), (*clause concerning the woman's portion*).

If I dismiss thee as wife and hate thee, and prefer to thee another woman than thee as wife, I will give thee two pieces of silver, that is 10 staters, besides the two pieces of silver mentioned above, which I have given thee as thy woman's portion, in total four pieces of silver, that is 20 staters. And I will give thee one third of all and everything which will exist between thee and myself furthermore (*divorce clause*).

The children which thou hast born to me and will still bear to me are the masters of each and everything that I possess and that I will still acquire (*clause concerning the children*) ..."

(Hereupon follows the detailed list of the woman's dowry stating its value).

"Total value of thy dowry, which thou hast brought with you into my house: in copper money three silver coins and four kite, that is 17 staters ... (*clause concerning the dowry*) ... I shall not be able to make an oath against thee on account of thy dowry, which is described above, by saying: 'No, thou didst not bring it into my house with thee.' Thy dowry, which is described above, thou hast brought it with thee into my house and I received it completely from thy hand, without a remnant. My heart is satisfied with it. If I should dismiss thee or if thou shouldst care to leave, then I will give thee the dowry that thou hast brought along into my house or its value in silver, corresponding to the price that is written, referring to this. I take it into custody" (after Lüddeckens, 33).

This example shows us that above all, the settlements represented an economic assurance for the wife. At times the husband has the right of using the wife's property, yet some agreements contain additional authority clauses, which grant the wife free usage of her property. Moreover, there are even examples in which the wife is entitled to dispose of her husband's goods. A change in the contract demanded the reissue of the whole document. A marriage settlement from the twenty-second year of king Amasis' reign was composed to replace an older one, dating from the fifteenth year of the same king's rule, because in the meantime children had been born to the couple, thus altering the property rights. Remarkably enough, one also had trial marriages for a certain length of time. It was possible to conclude settlements in reference to them, too. On an ostracon in Strassburg it is said:

"Year 16, third month of the second (or third) season, first day. Psenmin, son of Khensthot, the gooseherd, is the one who says to Tamin, the daughter of Pamont: That 2 (deben of) refined silver = 10 staters = 2 (deben of) refined silver again which I have already given to you before Hathor, (and) that other 2 (deben of) refined silver = 10 staters = 2 (deben of) refined silver again which I have given to you before Rattowe, (they) make altogether 4 (deben of) refined silver = 20 staters = 4 (deben of) refined silver again which I have already given to you before the goddesses. You shall be in my house, being with me as wife from today, year 16, third month of the second (or third) season, first day, until year 17, fourth month of the first season, first day. If it shall happen that (you) go away to your house without having come to the fourth month of the first season, first day, in my house, you shall pay the 4 (deben of) refined silver which are written above. If it shall happen that I be the one who has caused (you) to go, without your having come to the fourth month of the first season, first day, (then) I am to pay the 4 (deben of) refined silver which are written above, (which) I have already paid into the hand of the agents of Psenanup the money changer, the agent" (after Edgerton, 18).

Thus the man takes the woman into his house for nine months after having deposited the payable money with two agents, witnessed by the priests of two temples. It was the purpose of such a trial or temporary marriage to find out whether the woman could bear children to the man (1).

In general, the men wrote up the contracts for their women. Yet we know of two examples in which the woman is the author of the settlements. So it is said (Papyrus Berlin 3078):

"The woman NN, daughter of X etc ... hath spoken. 'Thou hast made me a married woman today. Thou hast given me one kite of refined silver ... as my portion. If I should dismiss thee as husband and hate thee and love another than thee, then it is I who shall give thee half of a silver kite, from this kite of silver, which thou hast given to me as my portion ... And I am separated (from thee concerning) everything whatsoever that I will acquire with thee, without carrying out any law-suit whatsoever against thee'" (after Lüddeckens, 33).

This settlement is instructive for us, since the woman

engages herself to return half of her portion and to renounce every share of the property acquired together in case the divorce should be caused by her.

We know just as little about the divorce proceedings as about the marriage act. Divorce was possible at all times. For the older epochs, we depend upon other indications, such as the effaced figure and name of the wife in the common tomb.

It surely cannot have been too difficult to obtain a divorce. The husband could "dismiss" his wife "as married woman" if he wished to remarry, or if his wife ceased to please him for some other reason, but besides returning her dowry, he had also to pay her a satisfaction. Nor did he have a claim to her portion. If he should not be solvent, the man's father would occasionally warrant with his property. As the contract cited previously shows, it was not difficult for the woman to obtain a divorce either. Of course, she only got back her dowry and perhaps a share of the property which they had acquired together, while the husband did not have to pay the satisfaction. Both could easily remarry later on. Nevertheless, the wife's property and the satisfaction in case of a divorce were only guaranteed as long as she did not commit adultery. In the eyes of the Egyptians this "heavy sin" was a great crime that could deprive the wife of her property and make her subject to punishment, too. We lack direct evidence of this except for one limestone ostracon in the Louvre, on which the oath of a woman is preserved. She states that during her married life "until this very day," she had not been together with any other man. In the end it is noted that the woman shall receive four talents from her husband (perhaps this is her portion) if she takes the oath.

Otherwise only two folk tales from the Middle and New Kingdoms, respectively, tell of a woman committing adultery. In the Westcar Papyrus, preserved in Berlin, which contains a collection of folk tales, a story is told in which the wife of a lector priest and magician commits adultery with a "commoner." When the deed is discovered, the man is condemned to death, the woman is burned and her ashes are strewn into the river. In the story of the two brothers, Anubis and Bata, from the Papyrus d'Orbiney we encounter the Potiphar motif (Moses I, 39, 7 . . .). Anubis' wife tries to seduce his unmarried brother Bata. When she does not succeed, she acts as if she had been beaten and tells her husband that his brother had attempted to violate her, but that she, as an upright wife, had defended herself; whereupon Bata had beaten her. In the evening when his brother returns from the fields, Anubis lies in wait for him, but Bata is warned by the talking cows and escapes. Bata then tells Anubis, who is pursuing him, the truth, whereupon Anubis turns around and kills his wife and throws her corpse to the hounds.

Before the Late Period, the Egyptian woman very seldom suffered such a negative treatment in literature. Otherwise she was always the faithfully caring wife, the princess with many suitors who must accomplish various deeds to win her, or the mistress praised by songs and poems. The number of stories which criticize women less favourable only increases during the period following the New Kingdom and in the Greek period. In the novel of Prince Setna it is a frivolous woman with whom he falls in love. But she claims his entire property and finally even the life of his children, giving as a reason that she is a priestess.

Herodotus (II, 126) tells the following story about Cheops' daughter: "Her father, who, on account of the construction of the pyramid, was in financial difficulties, sent his daughter to a brothel in order to pay his workmen with her revenues. She, however, had each suitor give her a stone, with which she supposedly built a pyramid for herself".

And in an Instruction of the Ptolemaic Period it is said: "Do not let it be known that your wife annoyed you. Beat her and have her take her property away . . ." (68) What a fundamental contrast to the solid world of the classic epochs!

We have mentioned before that motherhood was also highly revered in Egypt. One of the most important maxims of life for the Egyptians was that children be brought up to respect their parents. Thus, in the biographical tomb inscriptions of every period it is asserted that the mother and father had been honoured, their tombs installed and the mortuary service tended to. Frequently the parents, in particular the mother, are depicted in the sons' tombs, prompted by the desire of being together forever in the Hereafter. But the loveliest evidence showing the esteem a son had for his mother is presented by a passage from the Instruction of Anii:

"Double the food which thou givest to thy mother,
  and carry her as she carried (thee).
She had a heavy load in thee.
Thou wert born after thy months, but she was still
                  yoked (with thee, for)
her breast was in thy mouth for three years, con-
                  tinuously.
Though thy filth was disgusting, (her) heart was not
                  disgusted,
saying: "What can I do?"
She put thee into school when thou wert taught to
write, and she continued on thy behalf every day,
with bread and beer in her house.
When thou art a young man and takest to thyself
a wife and art settled in thy house
set thy eye on how thy mother gave birth to thee
and (all) her bringing thee up as well.
Do not let her blame thee,
nor may she have to raise her hands to the god
nor may he (have to) hear her cries" (after Schott, 50).

Not to have any children was a terrible and lamentable situation to the Egyptian, which he tried to redress through adoption. Nevertheless, witchcraft was far too often used in this respect. From the Middle Kingdom a statuette representing a naked woman with a child has been preserved for us in Berlin and bears the interesting inscription: "May a birth be given to your daughter Sh" (52). With this statuette Sh turns to her deceased father so that he may support her desire to have a child, since her marriage has remained childless so far. A custom that was widely spread at this time was to put little figures of naked women, often holding a child and made of clay, faience or limestone, into the tomb of the deceased. On the one hand, they were supposed to satisfy the sexual instinct; on the other, to

render possible the procreation of descendants in the Afterworld.

Considering the general respect accorded to mothers throughout the whole Pharaonic era, it is especially astonishing that representations of pregnant women are almost totally absent from Egyptian art. One of the few exceptions is the scene of mourning women in a doctor's tomb from the Old Kingdom, where a pregnant woman is depicted (Plate 18). This motif can furthermore be found on two official monuments of the Eighteenth Dynasty: in the temples of Hatshepsut in Deir el Bahri (Ill. p. 34) and of Amenophis III in Luxor. They tell us of the pharaoh's divine procreation and birth. From the New Kingdom some small bottles in the shape of pregnant women have been preserved (Plate 47b).

Although the Egyptians knew the connection between copulation and conception, the latter of which becomes first evident by the cessation of the menstruation, they had not yet recognized the actual biological processes.

Since the Egyptian very seldom mentioned it, we are insufficiently informed about the actual delivery assisted by midwives. Shortly before the delivery the pregnant woman, wearing a special hairdo, retreated into so-called maternity bowers – these were light edifices, which were easy to build and stood in the garden or on the roof of the house. She remained there until the end of the purification, which lasted for about 14 days after the birth (9). Representations of such maternity bowers have been found on numerous limestone ostraca in the artisans' settlement of Western Thebes. Pregnant women consecrated them to birth divinities, while some may also have been sculptor's models used for mural paintings. When the labour began, the pregnant woman squatted on two or four bricks so that the child was born near to the earth. It seems that later on this custom was given up and a special childbirth chair was used instead (66).

Considering the relatively high level of medical knowledge, it seems strange that there weren't any gynecologists in Egypt even though other specialists are known, especially during the Late Period.

The medical texts lack descriptions of both sexual life and

26

the actual delivery, but they do contain, among other things, recipes for accelerating the birth, staunching blood, as well as for preventing conception. In order to recognize pregnancy, the length of which could be exactly calculated, one used several methods. "The woman concerned has to drink pulverized Bededu-ka plant with the milk of a woman who has born a boy. If she vomits, she will bear; if she is troubled with winds, she will never become pregnant."

Another method to recognize pregnancy, and to find out at the same time whether it will be a girl or a boy, is the following: "Two pouches filled with emmer and barley are moistened with a woman's urine. If both grow, then she will give birth, if they don't, then she will not give birth. If the barley germinates first, it will be a boy. If the emmer sprouts first, a girl will be born" (after Grapow, 15).

Here the sex is determined according to the gender of the words; thus, in the Egyptian language, barley is a masculine and emmer a feminine word (66). Furthermore, the medical texts contain prognoses about the child's vitality, and suggest remedies against strong pains during the child's teething or against its excessive crying. "Remedy for stopping excessive crying: poppyseeds (?) of the poppy (?) and excrement of flies which is on the walls shall be made to a paste, shall be pressed and drunk on four days. Stops immediately. With reference to excessive crying, which means, an infant which is (constantly) crying" (after Grapow, 15).

We can see that apart from true medical advice and effective remedies, magic and superstition were rather important and especially common among women of the simple people. On the beds one attached pictures of the dwarf god Bes, who wards off evil, or of the hippopotamus goddess Thoëris, who was the patroness of all childbearing women. Amulets of these and other divinities were to render assistance to the women during their difficult hour. According to popular belief, seven goddesses, the Hathors, determined the newborn child's destiny. The baby's first sounds were supposed to show whether it was fit to live or about to die. A Berlin Papyrus with a collection of "Magic incantations for mother and child," from which we here give an example, contains regular exorcisms:

27

"Perish! You, who cometh in the dark,
  who creeps in
  the nose reversed, and his face turned back,
  who forgets what he came for! . . .
  Did you come to kiss this child? . . .
  I will not permit that you kiss it! . . .
  Did you come to harm it?
  I will not permit that you harm it!
  Did you come to fetch it?
  I will not permit that you fetch it" (after Schott, 50).

Names were considered an essential element of each person and to destroy them implied the loss of eternal life. Either they refer to wishes of the parents, or to the birth, or they have a theological significance. Therefore, they always have a concrete meaning and, apart from abbreviated names, can be translated. According to research, one may assume that the mother decided about the child's name.

Since the child was often nursed until its third year, wet nurses were generally employed in the upper classes. Frequently these women had great influence in the royal house and therefore acted an important part. Several contracts concerning wet nurses have been preserved from the Late Period, whereby the wet nurse engages herself to nurse the child for a certain period of time and receives an adequate salary in return, which was fixed from the first.

We quite often encounter the motif of a woman nursing in Egyptian art. Scenes of secular and religious spheres – the young king being nursed by a goddess – counterbalance each other. Representations of Isis suckling her son Horus only appear from the Late Period on. She becomes the prototype of a mother deity and even develops into a universal goddess. These representations are especially interesting in regard to the history of art and religion, because they probably furnished the model of the Divine Mother (Maria lactans, Plate 112) nursing the child Jesus of the early Christian works of art (42).

Mortal mothers with their children are depicted in Egypt at all times, in relief as well as in round sculpture. We have already mentioned the ostraca bearing scenes from the maternity bower and the figurines, which were given along into the deceased's tomb. A little ivory statuette of the Early Period in the Museum of Berlin (Plate 4) shows the interesting manner of carrying a baby, which can still be found during the later periods, but nowadays appears only among primitive races. By the child's sitting astride on the mothers hip, one could avoid the formation of a dislocated hip, which has become a widespread malady of the modern world. The intimate union of mother and child until the beginning of the second year is a biological necessity, which only exists among the Primates. It results from the fact that the nine-month period of gestation is followed by approximately twelve months of carrying the baby on the body, i.e., no longer in the uterus (11). Two copper miniatures of the Middle Kingdom, now preserved in Berlin and in Brooklyn, represent women who are sitting on the floor nursing their children. One of the statuettes shows a princess (Plate 26a), while the other was consecrated to the goddess Isis (Plate 20a). An unusual object, also in the Brooklyn Museum, is the alabaster figure of Queen Ankhnesmeryre holding King Pepi II, who is adorned with all the regal insignia, in her lap (Plate 16). A relief fragment of the Amarna period showing Queen Nefertiti nursing one of her daughters, must again be considered an exception.

The mothers carried their older children on their backs. While Egyptian women bundled their children in a cloth or in a part of their garment, the women from Syria, Lybia and the Negro countries almost always carried their children in baskets. Paintings in several tombs of New Kingdom noblemen depict such scenes (Ill. p. 28). The Negro women wore the strap around their forehead, whereas the Syrian women had it fixed around their left shoulder.

A description of a woman's role in the lives of her growing children should follow this account of prenatal practices and infant care. However, no material has been discovered on this subject, and an authoritative account cannot be rendered.

Queens and the Royal Harem

Woman's important position becomes most clearly visible within the royal government itself. Normally the queen, who, as "Great Royal Consort," writes her name in the cartouche like the pharaoh and possesses fixed titles, is not authorized to reign as "Pharaoh." But often the sovereign's claim to the throne of the two lands was transmitted by the princess, since she was qualified to inherit. This then led to the customary brother-and-sister marriages in the royal family. The crown princess was married to the king's eldest son, who, if possible, was an offspring from the pharaoh's union with the First Consort. If there was no son from this marriage, the sovereign's authority was mediated by the princess alone, and if she failed as well, the queen dowager as a rule stepped in. Thus the queen is of utmost importance for the continuance of the ruling dynasty. Although, in contrast to the pharaoh, she seldom appeared in public during the Old Kingdom, she more than once played an important part during this very epoch at the change of dynasties, i.e., when a male successor was wanting. According to Late Egyptian tradition, a woman apparently ruled independently for the first time towards the end of the Sixth Dynasty. During the days of foreign rule, the story of her short reign was still told, which Herodotus has transmitted to us in his historical work (II, 100). After the murder of her brother, Nitocris succeeded him in his office to avenge his death. For this purpose she had a large subterranean chamber built in which she arranged a feast and invited all the people who had participated in the conspiracy against her brother. Then she had the sluices of a secretly constructed channel opened and the room flooded, while she committed suicide to escape revenge. This is one of the fantastically embellished stories with which the Egyptians entertained each other and foreigners. But it lacks a historic basis, especially since research has cast doubt on the existence of this queen. Probably the Egyptian kings lists contain a transcription mistake caused by the misreading of a royal name (23).

During the Middle Kingdom the queen remained in the background, but after the Hyksos had been driven out of Egypt, towards the end of the Seventeenth Dynasty, she began to take an active part in political events. Perhaps the reason for this is the greater importance now accorded to the individual personality. Queen Tetisheri, wife of Seqenenre Tao I, became the ancestress of a new family. Her grandson Amosis, the expeller of the Hyksos, reports on a stele that he had a memorial chapel erected in Abydos for his grandmother. Tetisheri's daughter Ahhotpe must have been even more important, because, on a different stele, Amosis calls special attention to the part his mother had played. This woman was the first queen to bear the title "Divine Consort of Amon," which denominates the fictional wife of the god Amon. By this new office a princess who, as a rule, was the daughter of the king entitled to succession, was destined to be the wife of the crown prince and future sovereign. According to the myth of the divine birth of the successor to the throne, the god assumed the husband's figure and cohabited with her to procreate the successor. These conceptions were represented twice during the New Kingdom, once in the temple of Hatshepsut at Deir el Bahri and once in the temple of Amenophis III at Luxor. In practice, the result for the Eighteenth Dynasty was that the daughter inherited the office of the Divine Consort from the mother. For instance, when Hatshepsut assumed the king-ship, she passed on the function of Divine Consort to her daughter. Thus, the two offices were clearly separated, just as the queen's fortune was also separated from that of the Divine Consort.

The continuous bestowal of the office, in reality the inheritance, ceased when Amenophis III married a woman of common descent. In the Nineteenth and Twentieth Dynasties the title was given to several queens until towards 750 BC the office was subject to considerable alterations. From then on it was transmitted only by adoption and, since the husband was the god Amon, sovereign of Upper Egypt, the consort remained a virgin. The institution of the Divine Consort, which included an extensive administration, considerable estates and a large household, became greater than the powerful high priesthood of Amon, and a strong political factor in the Thebaid. When the Kushites came to Thebes about 750 BC, they forced the ruling Divine Consort Shepenwepet I, daughter of King Osorkon III,

to adopt Amenirdas I, the daughter of the Kushite sovereign. This way they "legally" brought Upper Egypt under their rule (49).

One of the famous women of Antiquity is Queen Hatshepsut, who was the only woman to occupy the throne of the pharaohs for quite a long period of time. As daughter of Tuthmosis I and his First Wife Ahmose (Ill. p. 34), she was the heiress apparent to the throne. After her father's death, she ceded the sovereign authority to her half brother, Tuthmosis II, by marriage. But when he died after a short reign, the sovereign rights passed to his son Tuthmosis III, who was the child of a concubine, but married to Nefrure, Hatshepsut's daughter and heiress. A table may illustrate the genealogical relations of the royal family:

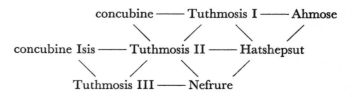

But Hatshepsut was not willing to content herself with the part of regent and queen mother. She soon had herself proclaimed "pharaoh" and assumed all the insignia of royalty, including a throne name. Since, according to Egyptian sovereign authority, only a man could become "pharaoh," statues and reliefs had to portray her as "king," in order to prove her claim to the throne. To be sure, some works do suggest her feminine character and combine this with the official attributes of the king (Plate 34). A still visible mark of her rule is the mortuary temple which she had erected in the valley of Deir el Bahri on the western side of Thebes. It was built against the cliffs in a series of three terraces, which was an unusual form of architecture in Egypt. One of the reliefs depicts the expedition to the fabulous myrrh country, Punt, where the Egyptian legation encounters the princely couple. The princess is humourously sketched as a corpulent lady suffering from muscular dystrophy, who follows her husband in clumsy motion (Plate 33). This scene attracted an artist of a later time so much that he copied it on a limestone ostracon (Ill. p. 32). On a different part of the temple walls the divine birth of the queen is represented. This is the first time we encounter this motif in fine arts. The inscription relates how Amon gave Thot the order to look for a young woman with whom he could procreate the successor to the throne. Then he announces his intention to the assembly of the gods. After having conferred with Thot about the choice of the princess (Ahmose, wife of Tuthmosis I) we read:

"This magnificent god came,
　Amon, lord of the Thrones of the Two Lands
　after having assumed the form of her husband.
　They (Amon and Thot) found her resting in the
　　　　　　　　　　　　　　beauty of her palace.
　She was awakened by the perfume of the god
　and she smiled at his Majesty.
　He immediately approached her and flew into a
　　　　　　　　　　　　　　passion for her.

　He lost his heart to her . . .
　His love penetrated her limbs.
　The palace was inundated
　by the god's perfume . . .
　His Majesty, this god,
　did with her whatever he desired.
　She delighted him with herself
　and kissed him" (after Schott, 50).

The following scenes show the pregnant Queen Ahmose led by two divinities (Ill. p. 34), and finally Hatshepsut's birth. Recent research has rejected the opinion to which scholars have adhered so far, i.e., that the cycle of images concerning the divine birth of the queen was made with the purpose of legitimizing her disputable claim to sovereign authority. It seems to be a ritual by which the birth of the successor to the throne, resulting from the encounter of the divine worldly sovereign with his consort, was consolidated by a sequel of scenes. By subordinating the previously autocratic divine sovereign to the supreme god (first Re, later Amon) – a change, which is apparent in the title "son of Re" from the Fourth Dynasty on – the king is replaced by the god, who procreates the successor after having assumed the shape of the sovereign (38). This "mythical" event is

32

superimposed on the ritual, thus our relatively late sources present a complicated picture (6).

The end of Hatshepsut remains obscure to us. She passed away after a reign of approximately twenty years, and Tuthmosis III was able to accede to the throne, which had been withheld from him for such a long time. Towards the end of his reign he had all of his predecessor's monuments demolished, her statues beaten to pieces, her name and representations hacked out, and the years of her reign added to his own.

Barely a century later we encounter another important queen. Against all tradition Amenophis III raised Tiy, a woman of common descent, to the rank of a "Great Divine Consort." We have already mentioned this royal couple on several occasions. Surely the two people were united by a strong personal love for each other, but more than that, it must have been this woman's prudence and energy that prompted the king to undertake such a step.

Judging by her portraits, Tiy was not a beautiful woman (Plates 44 and 59), but her traits do suggest a systematic and strong character. She took special interest in her husband's politics, advised him, and was cognizant of all important affairs of state. After the death of Amenophis III she received a letter of condolence from the sovereign of the Mitanni, Tushratta, where, among other things, it is said: "You know of me that I personally lived on friendly terms with your husband and how your husband also lived on friendly terms with me. And what I personally have written to your husband and what I have spoken, and also the words, which your husband has written to me, you yourself and my messenger, you know of it. But yourself know better than they, all the words that we have spoken to each other. Nobody else knows them."

With similar words Tushratta addresses the son:

"All the words, which I have spoken to your father, your mother Tiy knows them. No other person knows them and you can ask your mother, Tiy, about them" (after Wolf, 72).

The consort of this son, who received the royal name Amenophis (IV) and later called himself Akhenaten, was Nefertiti. Today she is known throughout the world by her limestone bust from Amarna (Plate 62), now in the Berlin Museum. The artistic colouring of this work has aroused the admiration of all lovers of fine arts. The question about Nefertiti's origin is still being disputed. She certainly was not a member of the Egyptian royal family, but one cannot prove that she is identical with the Mitanni princess Tadukhepa, whom Akhenaten had taken into his harem after his father's death. Only her name, which means: "The beautiful one has come," could possibly favour this old theory. Works of art of the first years of the Amarna Period (named thus after the new Middle Egyptian residence of the king) show the members of the royal family, especially the pharaoh, as being people of little beauty, since the portraits were meant to be "true." Nevertheless, it is certain that artistic aims are responsible for this, because Akhenaten used art as a means of making his religious reform universally visible (see Plate 57). The same applies to the family scenes, which – for the first and only time – show the pharaoh and his relatives in their private sphere.

Fortunately, the late Amarna works underwent a pleasant modification. Since exaggerations have been renounced, they are full of warmth, charm and perhaps real likeness to life (but Akhenaten is still portrayed as a remarkably ugly person). Nefertiti, however, must have been a beautiful and attractive woman in her youth (Plate 63). There is much evidence that she showed comprehension of and interest in her husband's enterprises. Yet, towards the end of the Amarna Period, discord broke out between them, but we don't know for what reasons. Neither do we know anything about Nefertiti's death, the place where she was buried, or the circumstances of her passing away.

From this marriage there were six daughters, and one of them, Ankhesenpa-aten (Plate 60), became the queen consort of Tutankhaten, who, after Akhenaten's death, left Amarna, transferred the residence to Memphis, removed the "Aten" from their names and called himself Tutankhamon and his wife Ankhesenamon. She became a widow after ten years of married life. Since the couple had no children, the queen dowager had to look for a successor to the throne by herself. Thus she undertook an unusual

33

step by communicating with Shuppiluliumash, the monarch of the Hittite Empire in the Near East, and asking for one of his sons as a husband. Ankhesenamen's letter has been transmitted to us in the royal Hittite annals:

"My husband died. A son I have not. But to thee, they say, the sons are many. If thou wouldst give me one son of thine, he would become my husband. Never shall I pick out a servant of mine and make him my husband."

Furthermore, it is reported in the annals that Shuppiluliumash was skeptical, since such a thing had never happened to him during his whole life and he dispatched an official to Egypt to find out the truth. Thereupon, the Egyptian queen sent a second letter, in which she wrote:

"Why didst thou say: 'they deceive me' in that way? Had I a son, would I have written about my own and my country's shame to a foreign land?" (after Güterbock, 24).

Thus the Hittite king decided to actually send her a prince, in view of the great possibilities this would present to him. An empire larger than any that had ever existed before was now close at hand. But the prince never reached Egypt. He was detained at the frontier by the Egyptian national party and murdered. Thereupon the queen had to marry Ay, a former officer and partisan of Akhenaten, who reigned for four years as Tutankhamon's successor.

Many years went by before, at the end of the Ptolemaic Period, a woman existed who once more tried to make national Egyptian politics. Cleopatra, the seventh queen of this name, and offspring of the Macedonian royal house, used all the means at her disposal to attain her goal. She was born in the year 69 BC, the daughter of King Ptolemy XII Neos Dionysos, whom the Alexandrians mockingly called Auletes, the flute player. At her birth nobody could foresee that she, the last woman of a dying family, would once more cause the Egyptian empire – which lost its last bit of independence upon her death – to be the ancient world's centre of political activity.

To describe her life, we unfortunately have to rely upon the statements and reports of contemporary persons who were either prejudiced or ill-disposed towards Cleopatra. In addition, Augustus employed her moral condemnation as a political means of influencing public opinion (2). He also

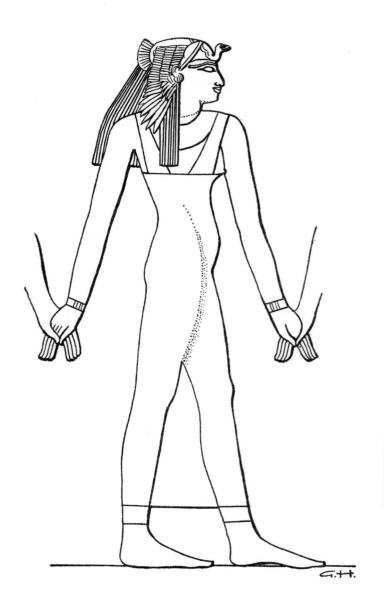

was responsible for the view that the effect Cleopatra had upon men resulted from witchcraft. In contrast to the legend which was formed soon after her death, the Ptolemaic queen was not a beauty (Plate 100 b), but she was far superior to her contemporaries thanks to her education. Cleopatra spoke several languages including good Egyptian, which was by no means a matter of course. Her wit, her charm and fascinating personality have made her one of the most famous women in history.

When her father passed away in 51 BC, she ascended the throne of the pharaohs, together with her brother consort, Ptolemy XIII. During the civil war, which soon broke out, she was driven out of Egypt in 48 BC, but she soon returned with an army of her own. In that same year, Alexandria was the site of the fatal encounter with Caesar, then the most powerful man of antiquity. According to the reports, she secretly had herself rolled up in a carpet and brought to Caesar by a confidant. Like many others, she charmed him on the spot. Caesarion, her first child, was born a year later.

In the meantime, Ptolemy had fallen in the civil war, whereupon Cleopatra was married to her next youngest brother, Ptolemy XIV, who was just eleven years old. In the year 46 BC the royal couple travelled to Rome with Caesarion to sign a treaty with Caesar. Cleopatra witnessed the assassination of the great Roman on the 15th of March, 44 BC, in that city. On that day all her far-reaching plans and hopes collapsed. All she could do was return to Egypt, where she had her brother consort murdered right after her arrival in Alexandria in order to proclaim the three year old Caesarion sovereign, under the royal name Ptolemy XV.

But soon another man attracted the interest of the twenty-seven year old queen of the Nile. He was Marc Antony, who had defeated Caesar's assassins in the battle near Philippi in 42 BC and thus had become ruler of the East. Though his mentality was different from Caesar's, he was equally fascinated by this woman, to the extent of renouncing his Roman heritage for her. Perhaps he had hoped to establish a new universal empire starting from Egypt, but, as a result, he risked and finally lost first his career, then his life. By his second marriage (40 BC), he was united with the step sister of Octavian with whom he had shared the Roman power. Nevertheless, in 36 BC, he married Cleopatra without having obtained a divorce from Octavia. When he finally did divorce her in 32 BC, he also broke with Octavian, who defeated his adversary in the following year in the battle at Actium. This proved to be decisive for the destiny of Egypt. The conflicts were drawn out until the year 30 BC and ended with the total defeat of the Egyptian army, whereupon Marc Antony and Cleopatra could only have recourse to suicide. Believing that Cleopatra had betrayed him to Octavian, Marc Antony threw himself upon his sword, while Cleopatra killed herself with snake poison. One could never prove the authenticity of the legend about her death caused by a snake's bite. Before her death, she had attempted to save her son Caesarion, who should have inherited the Egyptian throne, by sending him on a voyage to India. But Octavian cunningly enticed him back to Egypt and had him murdered. The three children born to Cleopatra and Marc Antony, a pair of twins in 40 BC and a son in 35 BC, were later led through Rome in a triumphal procession and given to Octavia to be raised. The girl, Cleopatra Silene, later became the wife of the Numidian king in what is today Morocco and thereby was ancestress of a new family.

After Caesarion's death, Rome's way in Egypt was free. Octavian made the country a province, which took an important position as granary of the Roman Empire.

Cleopatra's cults may be traced to the third century AD, but her fame rests upon what she accomplished as a woman. She won the love of the two most important men of her time in her vain attempts to preserve the dynasty and establish an empire in the East in connection with Rome. But in spite of her failure to do this, she was, nevertheless, courageous, clever, and energetic; she could flatter or be hard and inflexible, and she knew the stratagems of diplomacy. As the last queen on the throne of the pharaohs, she was not only a remarkable woman, but a patriotic defender of her country.

Up to now we exclusively dealt with queens in our exposition. Let us now have a look at the position of the king's concubines. In contrast to the "Great Royal Consorts," concubines and ladies of the harem seldom appeared in public. At times the size of the pharaoh's harem must have been remarkable, since the children lived and were brought up there as well. One of the sovereigns with the most children was Ramses II, of whom we know that he had at least 79 sons and 59 daughters. The royal harem had a special administration headed by a high official. In contrast to the oriental harems, the male employees were not eunuchs, but often married men. At the same time, women could also look after the ladies' well-being as wardens or attendants. As the name "secluded ones" implies the inhabitants of the royal harem lived apart from the rest of the court

household. In general, they were chosen for the pharaoh according to their beauty, so that women of humble birth could also be admitted. We know little of them, yet we learn in one case that even the daughter of a porter was among them. From the New Kingdom on, always more foreign ladies found their way into the Egyptian harems. Around this time, it became customary for the king to marry foreign princesses for political reasons – to seal alliances and treaties. Upon their arrival in Egypt they were given Egyptian names and taken into the harem with their entire court household. Thus they disappear out of our sight.

It seems to have been Tuthmosis IV who started this

Nubian Princess on Chariot
Being Pulled by Cattle

custom; we know that his son Amenophis III married foreign women several times. On the occasion of his union with Gilukhepa, daughter of the Mitanni monarch Shuttarna, a commemorative scarab was made:

"A miracle brought to His Majesty, the daughter of the prince of Nahrin Shutarna, Gilukhepa and persons of her harem, 317 women" (after Schott, 50).

Two years before his death, he married Tadukhepa, the daughter of the next Mitanni king. Her father gave her a considerable dowry, but in return, the Egyptian king had to make an even larger present in gold. When the princess arrived in Egypt, the king had just died. His son, Amenophis IV/Akhenaten, had her brought into his own harem, as every king took over the harem of his predecessor. When Amenophis III married the daughter of the Babylonian king, the latter asked for an Egyptian princess as a present in return. But he received the proud answer: "Since of old an Egyptian king's daughter has not been given to anybody." Usually the foreign princesses were only given the rank of a normal concubine, but Ramses II made the Hittite princess, whom he had married during the thirty-fourth year of his reign, a "Great Royal Consort," beside his wife Nefertari. On several commemorative stones erected in Abu Simbel, Elephantine, and Karnak the pharaoh reports that the sovereign of the Hittites, Khattushilish, wished to give his daughter to the "good god" as a "present of honour," because his country was in trouble. Then follows the description of the dowry, the voyage and the solemn arrival in Egypt.

"Thus His Majesty saw that her face was beautiful,
  the likeness of a goddess.
  The daughter of the prince of Khatti
  was beautiful before the heart of His Majesty.
  He loved her more than anything else,
  as something beautiful, given to him by his father Ptah.
  His Majesty had her name given to her Queen Ma'atnefrure" (after Schott, 50).

The task of the ladies of the harem was to delight their lord with dances and music or board games. The "adorned

King Ramses III
Caressing a Harem Girl

37

ones," as they were also called, were well-versed in many disciplines. Specially trained persons taught them in arts and music. Mistresses of dancing and choirmasters instructed not only the ladies of the harem, but also the ladies of high society. Thus the ladies at court and the princesses had to learn the use of at least the most important musical instruments; above all, the menits and the sistra, which were used in the cult. They also had to know how to play the lute, the lyre, or the harp to delight the divinity or the king with songs played in his honour.

Representations of the harem are very rare. Only twice is the king depicted together with a concubine (Plate 23) or a girl of the harem (Ill. p. 37), while one relief in the tomb of a nobleman from Amarna shows a harem consisting of two rooms (Ill. p. 38). During the course of Egyptian history, intrigues often occurred in the harem, but they were only referred to by allusions, since one was

afraid to let such incidents become well-known. Thus it is reported from the Old Kingdom that a high official named Uni was called upon, because of his especially trustworthy character, to conduct a secret case against Queen Weretkhetes, whose mistakes were concealed, however.

Conspiracies were also planned and prepared in the king's harem. In the Middle Kingdom Instruction of King Ammenemes I, it is conjectured that the assassination of the sovereign was plotted in the harem. Some of the preserved trial reports tell us about a harem intrigue during the Twentieth Dynasty that took on greater proportions. It was directed against King Ramses III, who fell victim to this attempt on his life. These reports of the proceedings are of special interest, since they offer a better insight into the life of that period than all official documents.

There were many foreigners in the service of Egypt, in fact, the whole bodyguard of the sovereign consisted of foreign men. They were better off than the people themselves, who, on account of the rising prices, mainly of corn, lived in misery. Most of the state's reserves had been exhausted so that it even had to owe the workers their rations. This led to agitations and strikes in Western Thebes. It was symptomatic of this period that the robberies of the royal tombs constantly increased.

A group of conspirators from the royal harem wished to take advantage of this situation. They were led by Tiy, a concubine of the king, who wanted to install her son Pentawert on the throne, and by the chief official of the harem. The reports of the proceedings show that they wanted to incite the people to rebel with the help of mediators. This is rather unusual, since palace revolutions were generally limited to a small circle, and the people were not consulted. This time, however, they speculated on the people's desire to rise up against the king, who was the cause of their misery. The conspirators succeeded with their planned murder of the king, but their pretender to the throne was defeated by the man who had already been chosen as successor, Ramses IV. He then ordered proceedings to be held against the insurgents before two special committees of trustworthy persons. On this occasion, an embarrassing incident occurred when it was disclosed that two judges had organized a feast with two accused women and a man. The unfaithful persons were subsequently punished by cutting off their noses and ears, while most of the accused were sentenced to death.

These few examples may be sufficient to illustrate the role of the woman in the royal palace by presenting a concise description of her life and work. Only a small portion of the many extant documents, however, could be mentioned here.

Clothing and Beauty Culture

In Ancient Egypt the desire to dress up was just as popular as it is nowadays. Nevertheless, women's clothing in general remained uniform and simple throughout the Old and Middle Kingdoms. The ladies of the high society, as well as maidservants and women of the lower classes, usually wore a long, smoothly fitted dress made of white linen, which reached down to the ankles and had two wide shoulder straps. The clothes, which were kept plain and seldom decorated, were sleeveless. A coat enveloped the body loosely (Plate 6) and provided protection against the coolness of the evening. At work the maidservants usually wore a kiltlike skirt (Plate 17a).

The dancers, who performed in the houses during the feasts, often wore only a short kilt as a sort of uniform (Plate 19). Sometimes two narrow straps were crossed over the breast as a decoration. One can only speak of "haute couture" in the New Kingdom. As we have mentioned previously, it was during this period that foreign customs and proverbial wealth flooded the country and brought about various changes.

At the beginning of the Eighteenth Dynasty, women still wore the customary simple clothes (Plate 37). But soon the dresses, which fell to the feet, were profusely pleated and, for the first time, the arms above the elbow were covered with short, closely pleated sleeves (Plates 67–69). Often one wore a thin chemise underneath the outer garments, which either were pinned together in front or knotted over the breast. Precisely at this time fashion, which was influenced by Syria, changed much faster than before. Garments differed in length, decoration, and borders, and the type of pleating was adapted to the prevailing taste. For this reason it is fairly easy to date statues and relief representations. The dancers and musicians, who performed during the feasts, even the maidservants, were occasionally completely naked now. Only a narrow belt worn over the hips (Plate 38) or, as among the acrobats, a piece of cloth wound around the lower part of the body (Plate 82), served to embellish and to heighten the erotic effect.

Just like clothing, the headdress was also subject to the change of fashion. In representations it is often difficult to distinguish whether the hairdos of men and women show natural hair or wigs, but in some cases the hairline is clearly visible underneath the wig (Plate 6). From the Early Period on, artificial locks of hair had been placed in the deceased's tomb.

On the other hand, the Egyptians greatly admired natural hair. This is proved by a series of recipes to help its growth and by discoveries of mummies, which have carefully groomed hair. Wigs, which had been used since prehistoric times, must certainly not be regarded merely as a method of enhancing beauty or festive attire, which no doubt they were. They also protected the head from the burning sun's rays, since they were in no way limited to gods, kings and noblemen, but were also worn by common people, servants, artisans, and soldiers. It cannot be proved whether, in addition to its profane use, hair also had any cultic significance. One of the most important coiffures of Old Kingdom women consisted of wearing the hair short and straight. This was customary among members of the royal family, the nobility, and among musicians and dancers. Representations from the Fifth Dynasty on show that maidservants wore the same hairdo. But coiffures made up of medium-long or long strands of hair were also common. Until the Fourth Dynasty they were worn exclusively by goddesses, women of the royal family and ladies of the nobility, but later on also by women of the lower classes. In the Middle Kingdom, short hair (Plates 23–25) and the medium-long strand wigs were seldom worn, whereas the coiffure of long strands became very popular throughout the different social classes. During the Twelfth Dynasty we first encounter the so-called volute or Hathor coiffure (Plate 27b): two strands of hair, with the ends rolled into volutes descend along each side of the head to the breast leaving the ears uncovered.

In view of the new style of living and the expansion of luxury during the New Kingdom, it is not surprising to learn that, like the garments, the coiffures became exaggerated and sometimes too elaborate. The long, formerly simple strand wigs developed into very artistic styles. The strands mainly consisted of thin plaited braids

Girl Playing the Lute

which ended in fringes (Plates 76a+b). Only in the period of Amarna did the queens also wear short wigs (Plates 56 and 69). Tomb discoveries have disclosed several wigs dating from the New Kingdom, which are mainly made of human hair, but sometimes also of plant fibres.

The ointment cone – a mixture of fats, myrrh, and other essences – came into use during the New Kingdom. Its task was to keep the wigs fragrant, and consequently it formed part of the beauty culture.

Of course, a person at work hardly wore a wig on his head, but rather pinned the hair together on the nape of the neck so that it wouldn't be disturbing (Plate 17a).

At all times it was possible to recognize the dancers by their special hairdo. During the Old and Middle Kingdoms long tresses falling down the back were characteristic. Small balls and disks were plaited into them, to make the hair swing better during the dancing (Plate 19). Later the coiffures of musicians and dancers were less uniform. A very unusual hairdo – perhaps for cult reasons – was worn by women in the maternity bower, where they spent the lying-in and purification periods (see Ill. p. 27).

As the representations – and other sources – show, hardly anything remarkably new developed during the centuries of the Late Period, neither in the intellectual or cultural sphere nor in fashion. On the contrary, one turned back to the past in regard to clothing and coiffure. Only when, with the Persians and the Greeks, more and more foreigners came to Egypt, the external image changed again. Slowly but surely more Hellenistic elements penetrated Egyptian life, as the works of art demonstrate (Plate 99).

Jewelry played an important part, almost more than clothing and coiffure. Besides its task of satisfying the need for beauty, it retained its former significance as a charm to ward off evil. Already during the Early Dynastic Period, when human beings were still buried in the crouched position, women wore pearl necklaces, bracelets or anklets made of bone or semi-precious stones. Later on metals were used to make pieces of jewelry – at first with copper, then gold, and finally silver, and bronze as well as faïence. The wide

collars were made of lapis lazuli, which probably was imported from Afghanistan, and of malachite, carnelian or faïence. Earrings were not known in Egypt originally. They were only taken over during the New Kingdom, from the Nubians and Negroes, who came from the south, and they were very popular among both women and men (Plates 59 and 77). Furthermore, finger rings were worn, which were made of cheap faïence or precious gold, more seldom of silver, bronze or iron. Hair ornaments were extremely popular, either in the form of simple circlets or artistically finished jewelry (Plate 43).

For the care and preservation of beauty, cosmetics had very early reached a high level of sophistication. This is manifested by the many palettes used to mix the make-up and other tomb equipment, dating from predynastic times. In the earliest lists of offerings it is considered necessary for life in the Hereafter to have seven kinds of oils and two different paints, one being green made of malachite, and one black, for eyebrows and lids, made of lead sulphide and sometimes of metallic antimony. The black paint was meant to accentuate the eyes, but, in addition to that, a healing power was attributed to it. It was kept in little jars made of alabaster or wood, whose beautiful forms still delight us today. Sometimes a line of paint was drawn from the outer corner of the eye to the hairline and to the ear respectively, and the eyebrow was lengthened accordingly. But it seems that the lips were hardly ever painted. Only one representation exists from Pharaonic Egypt of a prostitute painting her lips while looking into a mirror (Ill. p. 43). This is in the "Erotic Papyrus" in Turin mentioned previously. During the New Kingdom, the paint and ointment receptacles had especially beautiful forms. The cosmetics were kept in artistically manufactured vessels (Plates 75a+b). The objects, however, hitherto considered to be ointment spoons (Plates 48–51) served as offering utensils in the cults of the dead and the gods; their profane use could not be proved (69).

Painting and anointing oneself was part of life, just like eating and drinking, and it was as indispensable to the simple man as to the nobleman. For this reason, the workers always received a measure of ointment besides their ration

of food. And when, during the reign of Ramses III, the workers went on strike for not having received their rations, they demanded ointments in addition to food as the payment they were entitled to.

Numerous recipes and remedies for beauty culture have been preserved for us. They were written down in the medical scripts because cosmetics were considered a health curative. Many recipes are devoted to the hair. Remedies existed for or against the growth of hair, against premature loss of hair, or against its turning grey:

"Another remedy for making the hair grow, made for the Queen Shesh, the mother of King Teti: one leg of a female greyhound, one date stone, one hoof of a donkey; it shall be thoroughly cooked in oil in a Djadja-pot; then one shall anoint well with it" (after Grapow, 15).

A black bull's blood cooked in oil should blacken the hair turned grey; likewise, the dorsal vertebra of a specific bird, dried and ground tadpoles, and so forth. Furthermore, there existed recipes for removing hair, which were not intended for personal use, but were to be used on the hated enemy.

The care of the skin was equally important in order to keep it always pure and fresh.

"Another remedy for removing wrinkles in the face: rubber from the terebinth tree, wax, fresh behen-oil, grass from Cyprus; (it) shall be finely ground, (it) shall be put into a mucilage; (it) shall be applied to the face every day" (after Grapow, 15).

One recipe is introduced with the words: "Beginning of the book for making an old one young". Remedies against body odour are also numerous. Furthermore, there existed remedies against slackening breasts.

Like medicine, the Egyptian cosmetics were remarkably developed, because they were closely linked with the fight against sicknesses, and thereby were not limited to women. Nevertheless, many of the mentioned "remedies" were only magically effective. An abundance of implements – jars and bowls for oil and ointments, tweezers, spoons, combs, and so forth – were necessary for the beauty culture.

Handicraft, which produced remarkably fine objects in this field, reached its climax during the brilliant period of the New Kingdom.

Only little can be shown in this book, which is meant to give an impression, although incomplete, of the ability and the sure sense of form of the Egyptian artist and artisan.

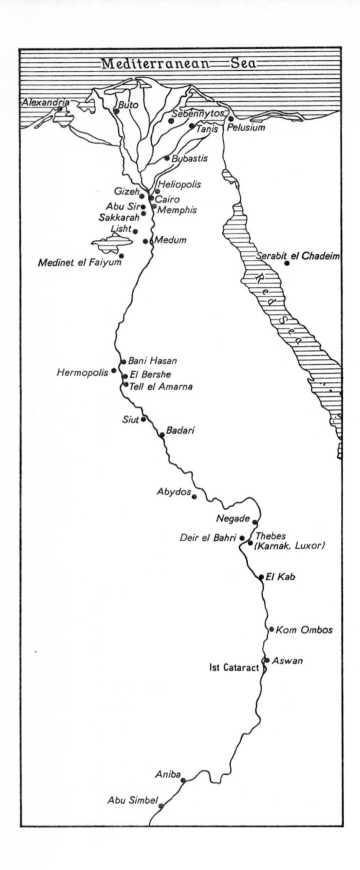

Comments on the Pictures

ILLUSTRATIONS IN THE TEXT

15 *Maidservant spinning*

Wall painting from the tomb of Khnemhotep at Bani Hasan. Twelfth Dynasty, about 1900 BC

19 *Astarte on horseback*

Limestone ostracon, height 10 cm. Nineteenth Dynasty, about 1300–1200 BC. Berlin, Staatliche Museen, Ägyptische Abteilung, Inv. No. 21826

20 *Woman vomiting*

Wall painting from a tomb at Western Thebes. Twentieth Dynasty, about 1200–1100 BC

27 *Woman nursing a child in the maternity bower*

Painted limestone ostracon from Deir el Medine. Twentieth Dynasty, about 1200–1100 BC

28 *Negro women with children*

Wall painting from the tomb of Huy at Western Thebes. Eighteenth Dynasty, about 1340 BC

32 *The princess of Punt*

Limestone ostracon, height 14 cm. From Deir el Medine, Twentieth Dynasty, about 1200–1100 BC. Berlin, Staatliche Museen, Ägyptische Abteilung. Inv. No. 21442
Caricature copy of the representation in the temple of Hatshepsut at Deir el Bahri (see Plate 33)

34 *The pregnant Queen Ahmose, mother of Hatshepsut*

Relief from the temple of Hatshepsut at Deir el Bahri. Eighteenth Dynasty, about 1480 BC

36 *Nubian princess on chariot being pulled by cattle*

Wall painting from the tomb of Huy at Western Thebes. Eighteenth Dynasty, about 1340 BC

37 *King Ramses III caressing a harem girl*

Relief from the High Gate of the temple at Medinet Habu. Twentieth Dynasty, about 1200 BC

38 *Representation of a harem*

Relief from a tomb at Amarna. Eighteenth Dynasty, about 1360 BC. After Davies, Amarna VI, Pl. XXVIII

41 *Girl playing the lute*

Limestone ostracon, height 13 cm. From Deir el Medine, Nineteenth Dynasty, about 1300–1200 BC. Berlin, Staatliche Museen, Ägyptische Abteilung. Inv. No. 21445

43 *Prostitute painting her lips*

Representation from the "Erotic Papyrus" in Turin. Twentieth Dynasty about 1200–1100 BC

PLATES

2 a) *Figure of a woman*

Painted clay, height 29 cm. From Mamarija, Period of Nagada I, about 4000 BC. Brooklyn, The Brooklyn Museum, Inv. No. 07.447.505
The figures of women with raised arms, birdlike heads and unformed legs, which are interpreted as dancers, are vastly stylized.

2 b) *Woman standing in a barrel*

Clay, height 18.5 cm. Supposedly from Nagada, 4000 BC. Berlin, Staatliche Museen, Ägyptische Abteilung, Inv. No. 13832–33
The woman, who is standing in a high barrel, is represented during the process of making beer; the necessary bread is being trampled on.

3 *Figure of a woman*

Clay, height 25.5 cm. Period of Nagada I, about 4000 BC. Bremen, Übersee-Museum, Inv. No. B 14506
The birdlike head, the unformed legs, and the hands raised to the head are characteristic of a certain group of female clay figures (see Plate 2 a).

4 *Statuette of a woman holding a child*

Ivory, height 7.5 cm. Early Dynastic Period, about 3000 BC. Berlin, Staatliche Museen, Ägyptische Abteilung, Inv. No. 14441

During the Early Dynastic Period numerous little ivory statuettes were formed, which show a mother holding her child. Later on this motif is abandoned. Here the mother has seated her baby on her left hip, supporting him with her arm, while she holds his foot with her right hand.

5 *Group statue of King Mycerinus with his consort Khamerernebty II*
Grey schist, height about 140 cm. From the king's mortuary temple at Gizeh, Fourth Dynasty, about 2500 BC. Boston, Museum of Fine Arts, Inv. No. 11.738
The couple depicted here is one of the earliest sculpture groups of Egyptian art. The queen embracing her husband is a motif which becomes canonical from now on.

6 *Statues of Princess Nofret and Prince Rahotep*
Limestone, height 118 cm. From Medum, beginning of the Fourth Dynasty, about 2580 BC. Cairo, Museum, Descr. No. 223
Prince Rahotep, son of King Snefru, and his consort, Princess Nofret, have been represented in two separately sculpted statues which come from their common tomb. The backs of the cube-like seats are almost raised to the top of their heads and form the background of the figures. Nofret wears a dress with straps and is covered by a coat. On the brow the natural hair can be seen beneath the short and heavy wig, which is ornamented with a decorative ribbon.

7 *Fertility goddess*
Limestone relief. From the mortuary temple of King Sahure at Abu Sir, Fifth Dynasty, about 2450 BC. Cairo, Museum, Temp. No. 6/12/24/9
A fertility goddess brings the sign for sacrifice and life on her arms.

8 *Group statue of Queen Meresankh III with her mother Hetepheres II*
Limestone, height about 60 cm. From Gizeh, end of the Fourth Dynasty, about 2500 BC. Boston, Museum of Fine Arts, Inv. No. 30.1456 (see also Plate 9)

9 *Queen Meresankh III and her mother Hetepheres II*
Painted limestone relief. From the rock tomb of Queen Meresankh III at Gizeh, end of the Fourth Dynasty, about 2500 BC
The representation of an Egyptian woman with fair (reddish-yellow) hair is remarkable and absolutely singular.
Hetepheres II (on the left) was the daughter of Cheops and an unknown concubine of the king. On account of the unusual hair colour, far-reaching hypotheses have been attached to this relief.

10 *Family group of the dwarf Seneb*
Limestone, height 33 cm. From Gizeh, beginning of the Sixth Dynasty, about 2300 BC. Cairo, Museum, Descr. No. 6055

Seneb filled many a public office and received his own tomb in the necropolis at Gizeh. That is where the sculpture group comes from, which has artistically succeeded in concealing the physical disproportion of the man and his wife, who was of noble origin. Seneb is sitting on the bench with his legs folded under him, in front of him the two children of the couple are represented. Physical infirmities are only depicted towards the end of the Fifth Dynasty and later.

11 *Group of the mortuary priest Thenti with his wife*
Limestone, height 65 cm. From Gizeh, about 2400 BC. Berlin-Charlottenburg, Staatliche Museen, Ägyptische Abteilung, Inv. No. 12547

12 *The priestess of Hathor Ihat with her mother Hetepheres*
Limestone relief. From the false door of Ihat, from the tomb of Nekaure at Sakkarah, Fifth Dynasty, about 2400 BC. Cairo, Museum, C.G.C. No. 1414

13 *Woman holding a fan*
Limestone. From the tomb of Nenkheftka at Sakkarah, Fifth Dynasty, about 2400 BC. Cairo, Museum, C.G.C. No. 1558

14/15 *Dancing women*
Limestone. From the mastaba of Akh-hotep at Sakkarah, end of the Fifth Dynasty, about 2350 BC. Paris, Louvre, Département des Antiquités égyptiennes

15 a) *Woman at a beer barrel*
Limestone, height 27 cm. From the tomb of Mersuankh at Gizeh, Fifth Dynasty, about 2400 BC. Cairo, Museum, JE 66.624

16 *King Pepi II as a youth, on the lap of his mother Ankhnesmeryre*
Alabaster, height 38 cm. Probably from Sakkarah, Sixth Dynasty, about 2200 BC. Brooklyn, The Brooklyn Museum, Inv. No. 39.119

17 a) *Women sifting corn*
Limestone relief. From Sakkarah, Fifth–Sixth Dynasty, about 2500–2200 BC. Cairo, Museum, C.G.C. No. 1546

17 b) *Maidservant grinding grain*
Limestone, height 34 cm. From the tomb of Weriren at Sakkarah, Sixth Dynasty, about 2300–2200 BC. Cairo, Museum, C.G.C. No. 114.
From the end of the Old Kingdom on, models of working people are placed in the tomb of the deceased and are supposed to provide for the dead in the Hereafter. The woman is grinding grain with a stone. Even nowadays the corn is ground in a similar manner among many nomads.

18 Mourning women

Limestone relief. From the tomb of Ankhmahor at Sakkarah, Sixth Dynasty, about 2300 BC

A section of a relief from the tomb of a doctor showing a group of women who are mourning the death of Ankhmahor. Among them is a pregnant woman who is being supported by two women.

19 Dancers

Limestone relief. From the tomb of the Vizier Mehu from Sakkarah, Sixth Dynasty, about 2300 BC

The girls, who are performing a semi-acrobatic cultic dance, are dressed only in a short kilt here. A disk or or ball is attached to the braided hair to give it weight.

20 a) Woman nursing an infant

Copper, height 12 cm. Twelfth Dynasty, about 1900 to 1800 BC. Berlin-Charlottenburg, Staatliche Museen, Ägyptische Abteilung, Inv. No. 14078

The Berlin figure of a woman, who is crouching on the floor and nursing her son, is one of the few copper figures of the Middle Kingdom. A similar object is in the Brooklyn Museum (compare Plate 26 a).

20 b) Statuette of a maidservant

Wood, height 85.5 cm. From the tomb of Meketre at Western Thebes, Eleventh Dynasty, towards 2000 BC. Cairo, Museum, JE 46.725

The statuette of the maidservant, who is dressed in a coloured garment, was placed in the tomb of her mistress along with many other models to guarantee the deceased's continuous provision in the Hereafter.

21 Semitic women

Painting on stucco. From the tomb of Khnemhotep at Bani Hasan, Twelfth Dynasty, about 1900 BC

The women belong to a group of Bedouins, who are emigrating to Egypt. The artist reproduced the peculiarities of the physiognomy and the external appearance very well.

22 Hairdresser Inenu with a lock of hair

Limestone, height 13 cm, width 25.5 cm. From the tomb of Princess Nefru at Deir el Bahri, Eleventh Dynasty, about 2040 BC. Brooklyn, The Brooklyn Museum, Inv. No. 51.231

In recent years the opinion has been held that the many depictions of dressing scenes from the Middle Kingdom, to which this fragment also belongs, as well as the representations of dancers and singers are connected with the cult of Hathor.

23 King Mentuhotpe II with a lady of the harem

Limestone, height 37 cm. From the chapel of a princess at Deir el Bahri, Eleventh Dynasty, about 2040 BC. Munich, Ägyptische Staatssammlung, Inv. No. 1621

The king is seated on a bench with one of his concubines and holds his left arm around her. This scene is unique in Egyptian art and remains without parallel except for Amarna.

24 Head of the sphinx of an unknown princess

Hard green stone, height 39 cm. Twelfth Dynasty, about 1900 BC. Brooklyn, The Brooklyn Museum, Inv. No. 56.85

25 Dressing scene

Limestone. Relief from the coffin of Princess Kauit from Deir el Bahri, Eleventh Dynasty, about 2040 BC. Cairo, Museum, Descr. No. 623

The representation is made in low relief and shows the princess during the morning toilet. While a man gives her something to drink, a maidservant arranges her hair. This relief is an artistic climax of the Eleventh Dynasty, above all, because of the careful treatment of the details – observe the position of the hands.

26 a) Princess Sebeknakht nursing her child

Copper, height 9.5 cm. Twelfth Dynasty, between 1900 and 1800 BC. Brooklyn, The Brooklyn Museum, Inv. No. 43.137

26 b) Two women with a child

Limestone, height about 6 cm. From Lisht. Twelfth Dynasty, between 1900 and 1800 BC. New York, The Metropolitan Museum of Art, Inv. No. 22.2.35

This little sculpture shows two women, one of which is arranging the other's hair, while the latter nurses her child.

27 a) Statuette of a maidservant

Wood, height 44.5 cm. From Thebes, Eleventh Dynasty, towards 2000 BC. Berlin-Charlottenburg, Staatliche Museen, Ägyptische Abteilung, Inv. Nr. 9536

27 b) Top of the statuette of a woman

Wood, height about 20 cm. From el Harageh, Twelfth Dynasty, between 1900 and 1800 BC. New York, The Metropolitan Museum of Art, Inv. No. 15.4.1

Here the woman is wearing a rather rare headdress. The ends of the two side locks have been tied together on top and rolled into volutes on the breast.

28 Statue of Princess Sennuwy

Grey granite, height 168 cm. From Kerma (Nubia), Twelfth Dynasty, about 1950 BC. Boston, Museum of Fine Arts, Inv. No. 14.720

This seated statue of Sennuwy, whose husband Hapzefa was prince of the nome of Assiut during the reign of Sesostris II, is over life-size and makes a sublime impression. She is sitting upon a cube-like seat which has no back support and both feet are placed firmly beside each other on the pedestal. The hands lie on the thighs and she holds a flower in her clenched right hand.

29 *Head of Princess Sennuwy*

30 *Statuette of Imeretnebes*
Wood, height 47 cm. Twelfth Dynasty, about 1900–1800 BC. Leiden, Rijksmuseum van Oudheden, Inv. No. A.H. 113
The statuette of this woman is unusual, her arms hang down straight against the body, while the legs are in a stepping position. The wig can be removed and covers the head as well as the neck and shoulders and accentuates the face.

31 *Group of offering-bearers*
Wood, height about 67 cm. From the tomb of the Prince Djekhutinakht at El Bershe, Twelfth Dynasty, between 1800 and 1840 BC. Boston, Museum of Fine Arts, Inv. No. 21.326
The single figures of servants of the Old Kingdom became groups in the Middle Kingdom. Here we see four people, a priest and three maidservants, who are bringing the offerings.

32 *Woman's head*
Wood, height 8.5 cm. From Lisht, beginning of the Twelfth Dynasty, about 1970 BC. Cairo, Museum, Descr. No. 4232
This charming little head from a female statuette was found near the pyramid of King Sesostris I. The wig was made separately, and the eyes were inlaid.

33 *The Princess of Punt*
Limestone relief. From the mortuary temple of Queen Hatshepsut at Deir el Bahri, Eighteenth Dynasty, about 1480 BC. Cairo, Museum, Descr. No. 452
Hatshepsut had the description of an expedition to Punt, the fabulous myrrh country, placed in her mortuary temple. The artist has admirably expressed the medical picture of the princess who is suffering from muscular dystrophy.

34 *Statue of Queen Hatshepsut*
Hard, marble-like limestone, height 195 cm. Probably from the mortuary temple of the queen at Deir el Bahri, Eighteenth Dynasty, about 1480 BC. New York, Metropolitan Museum of Art, Inv. No. 29.3.2
This over life-size seated statue represents Hatshepsut as "pharaoh" with a short kilt and the royal headdress, yet hinting at the female form of the body. This statue is among the artistically most impressive works of this period.

35 *Sphinx of Queen Hatshepsut*
Limestone, length about 100 cm. From the queen's mortuary temple at Deir el Bahri, Eighteenth Dynasty, about 1480 BC. Cairo, Museum, Descr. No. 6139
This work's model can be traced back to the sphinxes of Amenemes III, whose faces are surrounded by a mane.

36 *Nursing goddess*
Painting on stucco, height 18 cm. From a tomb at Western Thebes, Eighteenth Dynasty, 1450–1400 BC. Berlin, Staatliche Museen, Ägyptische Abteilung, Inv. No. 18534
A tree goddess nourishes a man, probably the owner of the tomb. A nonroyal human being who is being nursed by a goddess has not been found elsewhere in Egyptian art.

37 *Ladies at a banquet*
Painting on stucco, height 43 cm. From a tomb at Western Thebes, Eighteenth Dynasty, 1500–1450 BC. Berlin, Staatliche Museen, Ägyptische Abteilung, Inv. No. 15003
A woman who, according to her clothing and coiffure, may be the mistress of the house, gives her guests something to drink. The simplicity of the clothing favours the early Eighteenth Dynasty as this painting's period of creation.

38 *Ladies' orchestra*
Painting on stucco. From the tomb of Nakht at Western Thebes, middle Eighteenth Dynasty, between 1450 and 1400 BC
The group of three musicians depicted here is among the most graceful representations of female musicians. The outer two are dressed, whereas the middle one wears only a narrow pubic belt. The turned-back head and the legs shown in dancing position give the scene a special liveliness.

39 *Two maidservants decorating a lady for a banquet*
Painting on stucco. From the tomb of Zeserkaresoneb at Western Thebes, middle Eighteenth Dynasty, 1450 to 1420 BC
This detail belongs to a big scene representing a banqueting party. The two maidservants are naked wearing only a pubic belt around their hips. It is remarkable that the attempt was made to depict the maiden on the right in side-view.

40 *Banqueting party*
Painting on stucco, height 66 cm. From a tomb at Western Thebes, Eighteenth Dynasty, about 1400 BC. London, British Museum, Department of Egyptian Antiquities, Inv. No. 37986
The fragment of painting reproduced here shows the luxurious and splendid atmosphere of the big banqueting parties. On the top frieze we see servants and naked

maidens who are serving the guests; beneath a ladies' party is shown.

41 Ladies' party and young female musicians

Painting on stucco, height 61 cm. From a tomb at Western Thebes, Eighteenth Dynasty, about 1400 BC. London, British Museum, Department of Egyptian Antiquities, Inv. No. 37981
On the top frieze we can see a gathering of ladies; beneath, the maidens are either playing the lute or blowing the flute. They are also dressed beautifully, so that they are more likely to be young girls of society rather than professional musicians.

42 Detail of the coffin of Queen Merit-amen

Cedar wood, with inlay, length 314 cm. From Deir el Bahri, Eighteenth Dynasty, about 1420 BC. Cairo, Museum, Descr. No. 6150
Merit-amen was the daughter of Tuthmosis III and the consort of King Amenophis II.

43 Headdress of a princess from the court of Tuthmosis III

Gold with inlays of carnelian, turquoise and blue glass, height about 36 cm. From the tomb of three princesses at Western Thebes, Eighteenth Dynasty, about 1450 BC. New York, Metropolitan Museum of Art, Inv. No. 26.8.117
Originally, the headdress covered nearly the whole wig and consisted of 800–900 gold rosettes with inlaid ornaments. The head is a cast of a statue from the late Eighteenth Dynasty.

44 Head of Queen Tiy

Green schist, height 9 cm. From Serabit el Chadeim (Sinai), Eighteenth Dynasty, about 1370 BC. Cairo, Museum, Descr. 4257
This little head, which is identified by inscriptions in cartouches above the two serpents, bears a great resemblance to the Berlin head from Gurob (see Plate 59).

45 Princesses

Limestone relief, height 40 cm. From the tomb of Kheriuf at Western Thebes, Eighteenth Dynasty, about 1380 to 1370 BC. Berlin, Staatliche Museen, Ägyptische Abteilung, Inv. No. 18526

46 Married couple

Limestone relief. From the tomb of Ramosi at Western Thebes, Eighteenth Dynasty, about 1380–1370 BC

47 Two ointment flasks
   a) *Mother and child*
      Red clay, height 14 cm
   b) *Pregnant woman*
      Alabaster, height 12 cm

Both vessels come from the New Kingdom. Berlin, Staatliche Museen, Ägyptische Abteilung, Inv. No. 14476 and 24018

48/49 Four offering utensils in the shape of spoons

Wood, heights 22.4, 18.2, 18.5 and 13.2 cm. Eighteenth to Nineteenth Dynasty. Paris, Louvre, Département des Antiquités égyptiennes, Inv. Nos. 1737, N. 1750, N. 1733, 1748

50/51 Three offering utensils in the shape of swimming maidens
   a) Alabaster, length 22.5 cm. Eighteenth Dynasty, New York, The Metropolitan Museum of Art, Inv. No. 26.2.47
   b) Wood and alabaster, length 32 cm. Eighteenth Dynasty, between 1450 and 1300 BC. Paris, Louvre, Départment des Antiquités égyptiennes, Inv. No. 1736
   c) Wood and ivory, length 19.4 cm. Nineteenth Dynasty, between 1300 and 1200 BC. Moscow, State Pushkin Museum of Fine Arts, Inv. No. 3627

52 a) Seated girl

Stone, height 9 cm. New Kingdom. Berlin, Staatliche Museen, Ägyptische Abteilung, Inv. No. 14409

52 b) Statuette of the female singer of Amon Rannai

Wood, height 39 cm. From the tomb of Amenhotpe at Western Thebes, Eighteenth Dynasty, about 1520 BC. Moscow, State Pushkin Museum of Fine Arts, Inv. No. I. 1.a. 2099

53 Two statuettes of women

Wood, Eighteenth Dynasty, 1400–1370 BC
   a) Height 33 cm. Paris, Louvre, Département des Antiquités égyptiennes, Inv. No. E. 10.655
   b) Height 14.5 cm. Brooklyn, The Brooklyn Museum, Inv. No. 47.120.3

54 Women at the mummy coffins of their husbands

Painting on stucco. From the tomb of the two sculptors Nebamun and Ipuky at Western Thebes, Eighteenth Dynasty, about 1370 BC
The women are mourning the dead; one priest is making the libation, while another one (on the left) is performing the ceremony of the Opening of the Mouth.

55 Female mourners

Painting on stucco. From the tomb of Ramosi at Western Thebes, Eighteenth Dynasty, about 1380–1370 BC
The mourners are deploring the death of the deceased with lively gestures. The individualized representation of the figures indicates that during the reign of Amenophis III the artistic reformation of his son had already begun.

56 Lid of a canopic urn

Alabaster, height about 18 cm. From the Valley of the Kings at Western Thebes, Eighteenth Dynasty, about 1350 BC. New York, The Metropolitan Museum of Art, Inv. No. 30.8.54

The lid of this canopic jar shows the head of a princess from Amarna, perhaps Merit-aten. Later the inscriptions were meticulously erased, so that the urns – four altogether – could be used again. That the lids have the form of human heads instead of the usual divinities is a characteristic trait of the Amarna period.

57 Akhenaten's family beneath the radiating Aten

Limestone, height 32 cm. From Tell el Amarna, Eighteenth Dynasty, about 1350 BC. Berlin-Charlottenburg, Staatliche Museen, Ägyptische Abteilung. Inv. No. 14145

This altar painting comes from a private house in Amarna and shows the royal couple, on the left Akhenaten and on the right Nefertiti, caressing their children. The soft way of drawing the lines, the king's loose and collapsed posture, and the ribbons of the crowns floating in the wind are typical characteristics of the Amarna art. It is only conceivable during this period for the pharaoh to have himself portrayed in the private sphere of his family.

58 Two princesses from Tell el Amarna

Painting on stucco, height 33 cm. From a palace at Tell el Amarna, Eighteenth Dynasty, about 1350 BC. Oxford, Ashmolean Museum, Inv. No. 1893. 1–4 (267)

This fragment of a painting from a palace is part of a big family scene. Two princesses are sitting naked on soft pillows and caressing each other.

59 Head of Queen Tiy

Ebony, height 10.7 cm. From Medinet Gurob (Faiyum), Eighteenth Dynasty, about 1380 – 1360 BC. Berlin-Charlottenburg, Staatliche Museen, Ägyptische Abteilung, Inv. No. 21834

The little head belonged to a statue which was composed of multicoloured materials. The original headdress is lost. The features seem to indicate that foreign, perhaps Nubian blood, flowed in her veins. They express an energetic and determined character.

60 Head of a queen of Amarna

Hard sandstone, height 21 cm. From Tell el Amarna, Eighteenth Dynasty, about 1350 BC. Berlin, Staatliche Museen, Ägyptische Abteilung, Inv. No. 21220

In this head, which most probably is the loveliest one of the Amarna period and belongs to a statue composed of materials of different colours, we probably must recognize the future queen Ankhesenpaaten, consort of Tutankhamon. It was created during the later, more moderate phase of Amarna and is free of all distortions and exaggerations, which are visible in the head of the princess, on plate 70.

61 Statuette of Queen Nefertiti

Limestone, height 40 cm. From Tell el Amarna, Eighteenth Dynasty, about 1350 BC. Berlin Staatliche Museen, Ägyptische Abteilung, Inv. No. 21263

This statuette of the queen, who is represented as a mature woman, has not been completed. The paint has only been sketchily applied. The face, which shows rather hard outlines and firmly pressed lips, has a certain harshness that one can also observe in the famous bust (compare Plate 62).

62 Bust of Queen Nefertiti

Limestone, height 50 cm. From a sculptor's workshop at Tell el Amarna, Eighteenth Dynasty, about 1350 BC. Berlin-Charlottenburg, Staatliche Museen, Ägyptische Abteilung, Inv. No. 21300

On account of the good condition of the colourful paint the bust of Queen Nefertiti has attained widespread fame. Originally it was only a model for the sculptor so that he only laid in one eye in order to check the final effect. The bust as a form of art is practically unknown in Egypt.

63 Head of Queen Nefertiti

Quartzite, height 33 cm. From Tell el Amarna, Eighteenth Dynasty, about 1350 BC. Cairo, Museum. Descr. No. 6206

64 Princess eating a duck

Limestone, height 23.5 cm. Eighteenth Dynasty, about 1350 BC. Cairo, Museum, Inv. No. JE 48035

This sculptor's model has remained incomplete, because the artist's stone slab cracked. The motif – a member of the royal family eating – is only represented during the Amarna period.

65 Torso of an Amarna princess

Quartzite, height 30 cm. Eighteenth Dynasty, about 1350 BC. Paris, Louvre, Département des Antiquités égyptiennes, Inv. No. E. 25409

66 Torso of an Amarna princess

Quartzite, height 15 cm. From Tell el Amarna, Eighteenth Dynasty, about 1350 BC. London, University College, Petrie Collection, Inv. No. U.C. 002

The tender and soft forms of the naked body of a girl demonstrate that the torso, which is part of a family group, was created during the Amarna period.

67 Promenade in the garden

Limestone, height 24 cm. From Tell el Amarna, Eighteenth Dynasty, about 1350 BC. Berlin-Charlottenburg, Staatliche Museen, Ägyptische Abteilung, Inv. No. 15000

The tablet with the sculptor's sketch depicts a young royal couple. The queen holds out sweet flowers to her consort, who is languidly leaning on a pole. Both are dressed in beautiful garments and the ribbons are blowing in the wind. This motif and form are totally limited to the Amarna period. Later, the loose form rendered here disappears.

68 *Tutankhamon with his consort Ankhesenamen*

Detail from a shrine of Tutankhamon. Gilded wood, total height 49 cm. From the king's tomb equipment in the Valley of the Kings, Western Thebes, Eighteenth Dynasty, about 1340 BC. Cairo, Museum, Descr. No. Tut. 14

Scenes from the personal life of the royal couple have been applied to this shrine, which is only 49 cm high and was destined for an image of a god. The section illustrated shows Tutankhamon pouring water into the outstretched hand of his consort, who is seated at his feet.

69 *Tutankhamon with his consort Ankhesenamen*

Back of the throne seat of Tutankhamon. Gilded wood, with inlaid parts, height of the back about 53 cm. From the tomb of King Tutankhamon in the Valley of the Kings at Western Thebes, Eighteenth Dynasty, about 1340 BC. Cairo, Museum, Descr. No. Tut. 1

The throne seat of the king's tomb equipment comes from the period of his residence in Amarna and depicts the young royal couple beneath the radiating Aten on the back. The representation is used to prove that, in contrast to the restoration he officially carried out, Tutankhamon remained faithful to Aten, the god of his father-in-law, Akhenaten.

70 *Head of an Amarna princess*

Sandstone, height 21 cm. From a sculptor's workshop at Tell el Amarna, Eighteenth Dynasty, about 1350 BC. Berlin, Staatliche Museen, Ägyptische Abteilung, Inv. No. 21223

These princess heads, whose skulls probably were elongated by an artistic manner of exaggeration and indicate signs of degeneration, are among the most impressive works of the early Amarna Period. Originally the eyes and eyebrows were inlaid with different materials.

71 *Stucco mask of a woman*

Stucco, height 27 cm. From Tell el Amarna, Eighteenth Dynasty, about 1350 BC. Berlin, Staatliche Museen, Ägyptische Abteilung, Inv. No. 21261

The stucco mask was found in the workshop of a sculptor and served as model for the artist.

72 *Women dancing*

Limestone, height 40 cm. From a tomb at Sakkarah, Nineteenth Dynasty, between 1300 and 1200 BC. Cairo, Museum, Inv. No. JE 4872

The dance scene depicted here is full of swing. Women dressed in long garments are beating the tympanums with an increasing rhythm, while they sway to the time of the music. Two little naked girls, who are dancing to this, hold castanets in their hands. Their bodies, which are reproduced in lively motion and seem to be completely filled with the music, are very impressive.

73 *Detail of the relief of dancing women*

74 *Married couple*

Wood, height 32 cm. From a tomb at Western Thebes, Nineteenth Dynasty, between 1300 and 1200 BC. Berlin-Charlottenburg, Staatliche Museen, Ägyptische Abteilung, Inv. No. 6910

Amenemopet and his wife Hathor are sitting on separate seats, holding each other. Both are dressed according to the fashion of the time with splendid garments and wear artistic wigs.

75 *Two ointment vessels in the shape of young maidens*

a) Wood, height 16.5 cm. Eighteenth Dynasty. Leiden, Rijksmuseum van Oudheden, Inv. No. A H 116 a

b) Wood, height 13 cm. Eighteenth Dynasty. Durham, Gulbenkian Museum of Oriental Art and Archaeology, Inv. No. 752

76 a) *Face of a woman*

Detail of the limestone group of Ptahmai, total height 99 cm. Nineteenth Dynasty, about 1300 BC. Berlin, Staatliche Museen, Ägyptische Abteilung, Inv. No. 2297

This detail is part of a group of the priest Ptahmai, who is represented with his wife and children.

76 b) *Top of the statuette of a woman*

Limestone, height 50 cm. End of the Eighteenth Dynasty, about 1330 BC. Florence, Museo Archeologico, Inv. No. 5626

The face of a mature woman, who is already at the brink of old age, expresses personal experience combined with an intense deepening of the soul. The work has the features of a portrait and reveals the overrefined state of mind of the post-Amarna period, which has nearly become decadent.

77 *Princess from the court of Ramses II*

Limestone, height 73 cm. From the mortuary temple of Ramses II at Western Thebes, Nineteenth Dynasty, about 1280 BC. Cairo Museum, Descr. No. 741

This torso of a statue depicting a princess is very charming. On her head she wears a support for a crown, consisting of erect serpents. In her left hand, which she has raised to her breast, she holds a menit, which was also used as an instrument in the cult of the goddess Hathor.

51

78 *Statue of Queen Tuy, mother of Ramses II*

Granite, height of the original part 227 cm. Nineteenth Dynasty, about 1250 BC. Rome, Vatican, Museo Gregoriano Egizio, Inv. No. 22

79 *Goddess of the West*

Painted limestone relief. From the tomb of King Horemheb in the Valley of the Kings at Western Thebes, beginning of the Nineteenth Dynasty, about 1330 BC

Horemheb, who as a general under Tutankhamon had a tomb constructed for himself at Sakkarah, received a second tomb in the Valley of the Kings when he had ascended to the throne. Here he was buried. It is known as one of the loveliest royal tombs. The background of the polychrome low relief representations and inscriptions is light blue.

80 a) *Bowl with a female lute player*

Blue faience, diameter 12 cm. Nineteenth Dynasty, 1300 to 1200 BC. Leiden, Rijksmuseum van Oudheden, Inv. No. E XLII 38

80 b) *Queen Nefertari playing a board game*

Painting on stucco. From the queen's tomb at Western Thebes, Nineteenth Dynasty, about 1250 BC

Nefertari, consort of Ramses II, possesses a magnificently painted tomb in the Valley of the Queens. Here she is seated beneath a baldachin in front of a board game (compare Plate 83).

81 *Two women under a fig tree*

Painting on stucco. From the tomb of Userhet at Western Thebes, beginning of the Nineteenth Dynasty, about 1300 BC

This is a section of a painting which depicts a tree goddess giving the funerary meal to the master of the tomb, who is sitting under a fig tree with his wife and mother.

82 *Female dancer turning an acrobatic somersault*

Painted limestone ostracon, breadth 10.5 cm. Twentieth Dynasty, 1200–1100 BC. Turin, Museo Egizio, Inv. No. Cat. 7052

83 *Queen Nefertari*

Painting on stucco. From the queen's tomb at Western Thebes, Nineteenth Dynasty, 1250 BC

Nefertari was the consort of Ramses II. Her tomb in the Valley of the Queens is one of the loveliest installations of its sort, thanks to its beautiful paintings which are disintegrating today (compare Plate 80 b).

84/85 *Three mirror handles*

Bronze, Eighteenth Dynasty, about 1450–1350 BC
a) Boston, Museum of Fine Arts, Inv. No. 41.263

b) Height 30 cm. Berlin, Staatliche Museen, Ägyptische Abteilung, Inv. No. 13187
c) Height 26 cm. Brooklyn, The Brooklyn Museum, Inv. No. 60.100

86 *Woman mourning*

Limestone relief (detail). Twentieth Dynasty, about 1100 BC. Cairo, Museum

In a mourning gesture the woman holds her hand to her head. Dress, wig, and the style of the relief suggest dating the relief into the Twentieth Dynasty.

87 *Top of the coffin of Djedmutiuesankh*

Linen and stucco, painted and gilded, length of the whole coffin 170 cm. Twenty-second to Twenty-third Dynasty, between 950 and 750 BC. Berlin, Staatliche Museen, Ägyptische Abteilung, Inv. No. 32

88 a) *Married couple drinking water from a garden pond*

Painting on stucco. From the tomb of Neferronpet at Western Thebes, Nineteenth Dynasty, about 1250 BC

Neferronpet and his consort are drinking from the pond in the middle of the garden. Here the love of nature, which caused the Egyptian to lay out gardens and ponds, is reflected.

88 b) *Family of Inherkha*

Painting on stucco. From the tomb of Inherkha at Western Thebes, beginning of the Twentieth Dynasty, towards 1200 BC

Representations of pure family groups are seldom found outside of the art of the Amarna Period. Here we see the married couple surrounded by four naked children, who wear the typical coiffure of adolescents.

89 *The sky goddess Nut*

Painting on wood, representation on the inner side of the coffin lid of Hetepamon, length 170 cm. Late Dynastic Period. Heidelberg, Ägyptologisches Institut, Inv. No. 1015

90 *The goddess Neith*

Bronze with gold inlaid parts, height 16 cm. Berlin, Staatliche Museen, Ägyptische Abteilung, Inv. No. 15446

The crown of Lower Egypt worn by the goddess of war, Neith, is her characteristic headdress. From the Twenty-sixth Dynasty on she is also worshipped as a royal goddess since the main site of her cult, Sais, became of great importance as the new capital.

91 a) *Statue of a queen of Ramses II*

Green stone, height 55 cm. Nineteenth Dynasty, about 1250 BC. Berlin, Staatliche Museen, Ägyptische Abteilung. Inv. No. 10114

According to latest investigations this statue represents a queen from the time of Ramses II. It is not quite clear, however, whether it depicts Queen Nefertari (compare Plate 80b and 83).

91 b) Statue of the Divine Consort Karomama

Bronze with gold inlays, height 59 cm. Twenty-second Dynasty, middle of the Ninth Century BC. Paris, Louvre, Département des Antiquités égyptiennes. Inv. No. N. 500
This statue of the Divine Consort Karomama, contemporary of the kings Takelot I, Osorkon II and Takelot II, is among the loveliest bronzes. The figure was originally partly gilded.

92 The goddess Nut

Red granite. Lower side of the coffin lid of King Psusennes from the necropolis of Tanis, Nineteenth Dynasty, about 1220 BC. Cairo, Decr. No. 6337
The coffin was usurped by King Psusennes I. It was originally destined for the pharaoh Merneptah.

93 Statue of an unknown woman

Bronze, height 56.6 cm. Twenty-fifth Dynasty, between 750 and 650 BC. Berlin, Staatliche Museen, Ägyptische Abteilung, Inv. No. 2309

94 Statue of the hippopotamus goddess Thoëris, the patroness of pregnant women

Green stone, height 96 cm. Twenty-sixth Dynasty, after 650 BC. Cairo, Museum, Descr. No. 791

95 Woman and child

Limestone relief. 23.9 × 28.7 cm. Presumably from the tomb of Montemhet from Western Thebes, end of the Twenty-fifth Dynasty, about 650 BC. Brooklyn, The Brooklyn Museum, Inv. No. 48.74
The woman has her child wrapped in a suspensory cloth. She is sitting on a stool between two trees and has a bowl of fruit in front of her. Above, there is a damaged representation of two girls, one of whom is pulling out a thorn from the foot of her playmate. Both motifs are represented in the tomb of Menna from the Eighteenth Dynasty and appeared so attractive to the artist that he copied them from there.

96/97 Women picking and pressing lilies to make perfume

Limestone relief. From the tomb of Pa-ir-kap from Heliopolis. Thirtieth Dynasty, about 340 BC. Paris, Louvre, Département des Antiquités égyptiennes, Inv. No. E.11377

98 Upper part of a statue of a Ptolemaic queen

Schist, height 68 cm. Third Century BC. Berlin, Staatliche Museen, Ägyptische Abteilung. Inv. No. 21763

99 Offering bearers

Limestone relief, 35 × 53 cm. End of the Fourth Century BC. Berlin, Staatliche Museen, Ägyptische Abteilung. Inv. No. 2214
The reliefs of this tomb document a mixed style, which is characteristic of the symbiotic relationship of Greeks and Egyptians. Motifs and manner of representation are traditionally Egyptian, but, especially in clothing, strongly influenced by Hellenistic culture.

100 a) So-called Cleopatra (VII)

Limestone, height 27 cm. From the time of Augustus. London, British Museum, Department of Greek and Roman Antiquities, Inv. No. 79 7–12 15
The opinion held hitherto that this head represented Queen Cleopatra VII has become very questionable.
Probably it is the head of a Roman lady from Augustus' time.

100 b) Coin bearing Cleopatra VII's head

Silver, weight 14.72 g. Stamped in Syria or Phoenicia, 33/34 BC. Berlin, Staatliche Museen, Münzkabinett, former Löbbecke Collection (1906)

101 Mummy portrait of a young girl

Encaustic wax painting on wood. From Hawara, late First Century AD. Cairo, Museum, C.G.C. 33216
The portraits of the dead were painted on thin wooden tablets (sometimes on linen), added to the mummies and connected firmly with the bandages along the edges. This was not a general custom but was only practised in the Faiyum and a few other places from the 1st to the 4th centuries AD. Here ancient Egyptian tradition – the preservation of the face with a mummy mask, supposedly having the characteristics of a portrait – has been combined with the Hellenistic manner of painting.

102 Stucco mask of a woman

Stucco, painted, height 34 cm, length 62 cm. From Shech Abade (Antinopolis), Third to Fourth Century AD. Paris, Louvre, Département des Antiquités égyptiennes, Inv. No. E. 21.360

103 Woman tending to the harvest tasks in the fields of the Hereafter

Papyrus, painted (detail). From Thebes, Ptolemaic Period, Third Century BC. Berlin, Staatliche Museen, Papyrussammlung, Inv. No. 3008
The scene represented here comes from the Book of the Dead belonging to Tanetrudy, called Nainai. According to the Egyptian conceptions, one had to perform agricultural labour, among other things, in the Hereafter.

104 *Stucco mask of a woman*

Painted stucco, height 24 cm. About 100 BC. Berlin, Staatliche Museen. Ägyptische Abteilung, Inv. No. 24103

105 *Mummy portrait of a woman*

Encaustic painting on wood, height about 32 cm. Probably from Er Rubayat (Faiyum), first half of the Fourth Century AD. Richmond, Virginia Museum of Fine Arts, The Williams Fund 1955, No. 55–4

106 *Mummy portrait of a woman*

Encaustic painting on wood, height 43.5 cm. Probably from Er Rubayat (Faiyum) about AD 160/170. Berlin-Charlottenburg, Staatliche Museen, Antikenabteilung, Inv. No. 31 161,7

107 *Statue of the goddess Isis in Greek dress*

Marble, height 85 cm. First to Second Century AD. Berlin, Staatliche Museen, Ägyptische Abteilung, Inv. No. 12440

In the Greek and Roman periods, but chiefly in the Roman, the veneration accorded to the goddess Isis constantly increased, even outside of Egypt. Without any doubt, certain characteristics of this goddess passed on to the Divine Mother Mary (compare Plate 112).

108 *Bust of a woman holding a palm branch*

Painted limestone, height 26.5 cm. From Shech Abade (Antinopolis) about AD 320–350. Recklinghausen, Ikonenmuseum, Inv. No. 516

The bust shows a young woman, who is dressed in a long-sleeved garment and wears a bonnet on her head. Probably the piece was erected in a niche of a mortuary chapel.

109 *Tombstone of a woman called Koprous*

Limestone, height 38 cm. Probably from Terenouthis, Third to Fourth Century AD. Berlin, Staatliche Museen. Ägyptische Abteilung, Inv. No. 24141

110 *Head of the city goddess Tyche wearing the mural crown*

Inserted piece of cloth; woven wool on linen, height 17.3 cm. Third to Fourth Century AD. Moscow, State Pushkin Museum of Fine Arts, Inv. No. 1, 1a 5151

111 *Roundel with the representation of the earth goddess Ge in the shape of a young woman*

Woven material, linen and wool, diameter 25.5 cm. From Egypt, Third to Fourth Century AD. Leningrad, State Museum Hermitage, Inv. No. 11440

During the Christian Period motifs taken from Greek mythology were also used to decorate garments. Here we have the roundel of a tunica, which was coloured black, white, yellow, orange, pink, brown, purple, dark-blue and light blue.

112 *The Divine Mother nursing her child (Maria lactans)*

Limestone, height 55 cm. From Medinet el Faiyum, Fifth to Sixth Century AD. Berlin, Staatliche Museen, Frühchristlich-byzantinische Abteilung, Inv. No. 4726

The motif of the Divine Mother nursing her child, which is very current in Pharaonic art, has been transformed and taken over on the tomb stelae of the Early Christian (Coptic) Period.

Chronology

Before 5000	*Paleolithic Period*	
5000–4000	*Neolithic Period*	
		Lower Egypt:
		cultures of Merimde-Beni Salame,
		El Omari and Faiyum
		Upper Egypt:
		Tasian culture
after 4000	*Chalcolithic Period*	
		Upper Egypt:
		Badarian culture, Naqada I
after 3300		Entire Egypt:
		Naqada II
2950–2660	*Early Dynastic Period* (Thinite Period)	
	First and Second Dynasties	
2660–2134	*Old Kingdom*	
2660–2590		Third Dynasty
		Djoser
2590–2470		Fourth Dynasty
		Sneferu
		Cheops
		Chephren
		Mycerinus
2470–2320		Fifth Dynasty
		Userkaf
		Sahure
		Nyuserre
		Unas
2320–2160		Sixth Dynasty
		Teti
		Pepi I and II
		Merenre I and II
		"Nitocris"
2160–2134		Seventh and Eighth Dynasties
2134–2040	*First Intermediate Period* (Heracleopolitan Period)	
	Ninth and Tenth Dynasties	
	(Herakleopolis)	
	Eleventh Dynasty, First Half (Thebes)	
	Mentuhotpe I and II	
2040–1660	*Middle Kingdom*	

2040	Reunification of Egypt by Mentuhotpe II	
	of Thebes	
2040–1991	Eleventh Dynasty, Second Half (Thebes)	
		Mentuhotpe II and III
1991–1785		Twelfth Dynasty
		Sesostris I–III
		Amenemes I–IV
1785–1660		Thirteenth and Fourteenth Dynasties
		Numerous kings succeeding each other
		rapidly
1660–1555	*Second Intermediate Period* (Hyksos Period)	
1660–1550		Fifteenth and Sixteenth Dynasties of the
		Hyksos Rulers
1660–1555		Seventeenth Dynasty (Thebes)
1555–1085	*New Kingdom*	
1555*–1306		Eighteenth Dynasty
		Amosis
		Tuthmosis I and II
1490–1468		Hatshepsut
1490–1436		Tuthmosis III
1438–1412		Amenophis II
1412–1402		Tuthmosis IV
1402–1364		Amenophis III
1364–1347		Amenophis IV / Akhenaten
1347–1338		Tutankhamon
1338–1334		Ay
1334–1306		Horemheb
1306–1186		Nineteenth Dynasty
		Ramses I
		Seti I
1290–1224		Ramses II
1224–1204		Merneptah
		Seti II

*Mean value. Von Beckerath puts the beginning of the Eighteenth
Dynasty at 1557, and Hornung at 1552.

1186–1085	Twentieth Dynasty	
	Ramses III through XI	
1085–730	*Third Intermediate Period*	
1085–950	Twenty-first Dynasty (Tanis)	
	in Upper Egypt existed the Divine State of Amon	
950–730	Twenty-second and Twenty-third Dynasties (Libyans)	
	Libyan kings named Sheshonq, Osorkon, Takelot	
730–715	Twenty-fourth Dynasty (Sais)	
730–332	*Late Dynastic Period*	
751–656	Twenty-fifth Dynasty (Kushite Period)	
	Kashta	
	Piankhi	
about 730	*In the twenty-first year of his reign Piankhi conquers Lower Egypt*	
	Shabaqa	
	Taharqa	
	Tanwetamani	
664–525	Twenty-sixth Dynasty (Saite Period)	
	Psametik I	
	Necho II	
	Apries	
	Amasis	

525–404	Twenty-seventh Dynasty (First Persian Period)	
	Cambyses	
	Darius	
	Xerxes	
404–341	Twenty-eighth through Thirtieth Dynasties	
	Nectanebos I and II	
341–332	Thirty-first Dynasty (Second Persian Period)	
332–30	*Greek Period*	
332	*Conquest of Egypt by Alexander the Great*	
332–323	Alexander the Great	
323–304	*Diadochi fights*	
304–30	Ptolemy I through XIV	
	Cleopatra VII	
30 BC	*Egypt becomes Roman province*	
30 BC–AD 395	*Roman Period*	
AD 395	*When the Roman Empire is divided, Egypt falls under Byzantine rule*	
641	*Arabian Conquest of Egypt*	

The dates proposed for the Early Dynastic Period
and the Old Kingdom correspond to the
chronology of von Beckerath (1961).
For the statements concerning the
New Kingdom I have followed Hornung (1964).
Only the most important kings have
been mentioned by their names.

Bibliography

1 Adams, B., *Paramoné und verwandte Texte.*
Studien zum Dienstvertrag im Lichte der Papyri. Berlin, 1964.

2 Becher, I., *Das Bild der Kleopatra in der griechischen und latei-nischen Literatur.* Berlin, 1966.

3 Blackman, A. M., "On the Position of Women in the Ancient Egyptian Hierarchy", *JEA* Vol. 7, 1921, pp. 8 ff.

4 Bonnet, H., *Reallexikon der ägyptischen Religionsgeschichte.* Berlin, 1952.

5 Bringmann, L., *Die Frau im ptolemäisch-kaiserlichen Ägypten.* Bonn, 1939.

6 Brunner, H., "Die Geburt des Gottkönigs. Studien zur Über-lieferung eines altägyptischen Mythos", *Ägyptologische Ab-handlungen*, Vol. 10, Wiesbaden, 1964.

7 Brunner, H., "Eine neue Amarna-Prinzessin," *ÄZ* Vol. 74, 1938, pp. 104 ff.

8 Brunner, H., *Altägyptische Erziehung*, Wiesbaden, 1957.

9 Brunner-Traut, E., "Die Wochenlaube," *Mitteilungen des In-stituts für Orientforschung*, Vol. III, Berlin, 1955, pp. 11 ff.

10 Brunner-Traut, E., "Der Tanz im Alten Ägypten," *Ägypto-logische Forschungen*, Vol. 6, Glückstadt, 1938.

11 v. Büschelberger, H., "Luxationshüfte", *Orthopädie* Vol. 8, 1964.

12 Černý, J., "The Will of Naunakhte and the Related Docu-ments," *JEA* Vol. 31, 1945, pp. 29 ff.

13 Černý, J., "Consanguineous Marriage in Pharaonic Egypt," *JEA* Vol. 40, 1954, pp. 23 ff.

14 Černý, J., and Peet, T. E., "A Marriage Settlement of the Twentieth Dynasty (Papyrus Turin 2021)," *JEA* Vol. 13, 1927, pp. 30 ff.

15 v. Deines, H., Grapow, H., Westendorf, W., *Übersetzung der medizinischen Texte. Grundriß der Medizin der Alten Ägypter*, Vol. IV, 1. Berlin, 1958.

16 Desroches-Noblecourt, Chr., "'Concubines du Mort' et mères de famille au moyen Empire," *BIFAO* Vol. 53, 1953, pp. 7 ff.

17 Edel, E., "Weitere Briefe aus der Heiratskorrespondenz Ramses II," in: *Geschichte des Alten Testaments, Beiträge zur historischen Theologie*, Vol. 16, 1953, pp. 29 ff.

18 Edgerton, W. F., *Notes on Egyptian Marriage Chiefly in the Ptolemaic Period.* Chicago, 1931.

19 Erman, A., *Die Literatur der Ägypter*, Leipzig, 1923.

20 Erman, A., and Ranke, H., *Ägypten und ägyptisches Leben im Altertum.* Tübingen, 1923.

21 Gardiner, A. H., "Adoption Extraordinary," *JEA* Vol. 26, 1940, pp. 23 ff.

22 Gauthier-Laurent, M., "Les scènes de coiffure féminine dans l'ancienne Egypte," *Mélanges Maspero*, Vol. I, Cairo 1935–38, pp. 673 ff.

23 Goedicke, H., "Zur Chronologie der sogenannten 'Ersten Zwischenzeit'," *ZDMG* Vol. 112, 1966, pp. 239 ff. (con-cerning the problem of "Nitocris").

24 Güterbock, H. G., "The Deeds of Suppiluliuma as Told by his Son, Mursili II," *Journal of Cuneiform Studies*, Vol. X, New Haven, 1956, pp. 94 ff.

25 Hermann, A., *Beiträge zur Erklärung der ägyptischen Liebes-dichtung. Grapow-Festschrift*, Berlin, 1955, pp. 118 ff.

26 Hermann, A., *Altägyptische Liebesdichtung.* Wiesbaden, 1959.

27 Hermann, A., "Das Kind und seine Hüterin," *Mitteilungen des Deutschen Instituts für Ägypt. Altertumskunde in Kairo*, Vol. 8, Berlin, 1939, pp. 171 ff.

28 Herodot, *Historien.* Deutsche Gesamtausgabe übersetzt von A. Hornefer, neu herausgegeben und erläutert von H. W. Haussig, Stuttgart, 1955.

29 Kaplony-Heckel, U., "Die demotischen Tempeleide," *Ägyptologische Abhandlungen*, Vol. 6, Wiesbaden, 1963.

30 Kees, H., *Das Alte Ägypten*, München, 1933.

31 Leipoldt, J., *Die Frau in der antiken Welt und im Urchristentum*, third edition with a preface by S. Morenz, Leipzig, 1965.

32 de Linage, J., "L'acte d'établissement et le contrat de mariage d'un esclave sous Thoutmès III." *BIFAO*, Vol. 38, 1939, pp. 217 ff.

33 Lüddeckens, E., "Ägyptische Eheverträge," *Ägyptologische Abhandlungen*, Vol. I. Wiesbaden, 1960.

34 De Meulenaere, H., "De Vrouw in de Laat-Egyptische Autobiografie," *Phoenix*, Leiden, Vol. 8, 1962, pp. 134 ff.

35 Middleton, R., "Brother-Sister and Father-Daughter Mar-riage in Ancient Egypt," *American Sociological Review*, Vol. 27, 1962, pp. 603 ff.

36 Modrzejewski, J., "Die Geschwisterehe in der hellenistischen Praxis und nach römischem Recht," *Zeitschrift der Savigny-Stiftung, Romanistische Abteilung*, Vol. 81, 1964, pp. 52 ff.

37 Morenz, S., "Der alte Orient. Von Bedeutung und Struktur seiner Geschichte," *Propyläen-Weltgeschichte*, Vol. 11, Berlin, 1965, pp. 27 ff.

38 Morenz, S., "Die Geburt des ägyptischen Gottkönigs," *Forschungen und Fortschritte*, Vol. 40, No. 12, Berlin, 1966, pp. 366 ff.

39 Morenz, S., "Eine Wöchnerin mit Siegelring," *ÄZ*, Vol. 83, 1958.

40 Müller, Chr., *Die Frauenfrisur im Alten Ägypten.* Unpublished doctoral dissertation, Leipzig, 1960

41 Müller, D., "Die Zeugung durch das Herz in Religion und Medizin der Ägypter," *Orientalia*, Vol. 35, 1966, pp. 247 ff.

42 Müller, H. W., "Die stillende Gottesmutter in Ägypten," *Materia Medica Nordmark*, 2. Sonderheft, Hamburg, 1963.

43 Müller, W. M., *Die Liebespoesie der Alten Ägypter.* Leipzig, 1899.

44 Nietzold, J., *Die Ehe in Ägypten zur ptolemäisch-römischen Zeit.* Leipzig, 1903. (outdated)

45 Parker, R. A., "A Late Demotic Gardening Agreement. Medinet Habu Ostracon 4038," *JEA*, Vol. 26, 1940, pp. 84 ff.

46 Pestman, P. W., *Marriage and Matrimonial Property in Ancient Egypt*, Leiden, 1961.

47 Ranke, H., "Ein ägyptisches Relief in Princeton," *Journal of Near Eastern Studies.* Vol. 9, Chicago, 1950, pp. 228 ff.

48 Riefstahl, E., "Two Hairdressers of the Eleventh Dynasty," *Journal of Near Eastern Studies*, Vol. 15, Chicago, 1956, pp. 10 ff.

49 Sander-Hansen, C. E., *Das Gottesweib des Amun.* Copenhagen, 1940.

50 Schott, S., *Altägyptische Liebeslieder.* Zürich, 1950.

51 Schott, S., "Ein Fall von Prüderie aus der Ramessidenzeit," *ÄZ*, Vol. 75, 1939, pp. 100 ff.

52 Schott, S., "Die Bitte um ein Kind auf einer Grabfigur des frühen Mittleren Reiches," *JEA*, Vol. 16, 1930, p. 23.

53 Seidl, E., "Einführung in die ägyptische Rechtsgeschichte bis zum Ende des Neuen Reiches," *Ägyptologische Forschungen*, Vol. 10, 2nd ed., Glückstadt, 1951.

54 Seidl, E., "Ägyptische Rechtsgeschichte der Saiten- und Perserzeit," *Ägyptologische Forschungen*, Vol. 20, Glückstadt, 1956.

55 Seidl, E., "Ptolemäische Rechtsgeschichte," *Ägyptologische Forschungen*, Vol. 22, 2nd ed., Glückstadt, 1962.

56 Sethe, K., "Das Fehlen des Begriffes der Blutschande bei den alten Ägyptern," *ÄZ*, Vol. 50, 1912, pp. 57 ff.

57 Sethe, K., "Zum Inzest des Snofru," *ÄZ*, Vol. 54, 1918, pp. 54 ff.

58 Smither, P., "The Report Concerning the Slave Girl Senbet," *JEA*, Vol. 34, London, 1948, pp. 31–34.

59 Spiegel, J., "Poesie und Satire," in: *Handbuch der Orientalistik*, Vol. I, Chapter 2, Leiden, 1952.

60 Spiegelberg, W., "Wie weit läßt sich der Brauch des formulierten Ehevertrages in Ägypten zurückverfolgen?" *ÄZ*, Vol. 55, 1918, pp. 94 ff.

61 Spiegelberg, W., "Note on the feminine character of the New Empire," *JEA*, Vol. 15, 1929, p. 199.

62 Staehelin, E., "Untersuchungen zur ägyptischen Tracht im Alten Reich," *Münchner Ägyptologische Studien*, Vol. 8, Munich, 1966.

63 Tanner, R., "Untersuchungen zur Rechtsstellung der Frau im pharaonischen Ägypten," *KLIO*, Vol. 45, 1966 and Vol. 46, 1967.

64 Thierfelder, H., *Die Geschwisterehe im hellenistisch-römischen Ägypten.* Münster, 1960.

65 Thompson, Sir Herbert, "Two Demotic Self-Dedications," *JEA*, Vol. 26, London, 1940, pp. 68 ff.

66 Unger, R., *Die Mutter mit dem Kinde in Ägypten.* Unpublished dissertation, Leipzig, 1957.

67 Vercoutter, J., "Les femmes et l'amour au temps des Pharaons," in: *Miroir de l'Histoire*, 186, June 1965, pp. 32 ff.

68 Volten, A., "Die moralische Lehre des demotischen Papyrus Louvre 2414," *Studi in onore dei J. Rosellini*, Vol. II, Pisa, 1955, pp. 269 ff.

69 Wallert, I., "Der verzierte Löffel," *Ägyptologische Abhandlungen*, Vol. 16, Wiesbaden, 1967.

70 Weindler, F., *Geburts- und Wochenbettdarstellungen auf altägyptischen Tempelreliefs.* Munich, 1915.

71 Wiedemann, A., *Das alte Ägypten.* Heidelberg, 1920.

72 Wolf, W., *Kulturgeschichte des Alten Ägypten.* Kröner-Verlag, Stuttgart, 1962.

73 Wolf, W., *Die Kunst Ägyptens.* Stuttgart, 1957.

74 Young, E., "A Possible Consanguineous Marriage in the Time of Philip Arrhidaeus," *Journal of the American Research Center of Egypt*, Vol. IV, Boston, 1965, pp. 69 ff.

Abbreviations

ÄZ   Zeitschrift für ägyptische Sprache und Altertumskunde, Leipzig

BIFAO   Bulletin de l'Institut Français d'Archéologie Orientale, Cairo

JEA   Journal of Egyptian Archaeology, London

ZDMG   Zeitschrift der Deutschen Morgenländischen Gesellschaft, Wiesbaden

Sources of Illustrations

Ägyptische Staatssammlung, Munich: 23

Ashmolean Museum, Oxford: 58

Bildarchiv Foto Marburg: 12–15, 17a, 46, 78, 94, 101

British Museum, Department of Egyptian Antiquities, London: 40, 41

British Museum, Department of Greek and Roman Antiquities, London: 100a

Brooklyn Museum, Brooklyn: 2a, 16, 22, 24, 26a, 53a, 84/85c, 95

Burges, A., Munich: 9, 32, 38, 79, 80b, 88a

Feucht, E., Heidelberg: 54

Forman, W., Prague: 7, 33, 35, 44, 72, 73, 77, 86

Gulbenkian Museum of Oriental Art and Archaeology, Durham: 75b

Hirmer-Verlag, Munich: 39, 42, 55, 63, 68, 69, 83, 92

Ikonen-Museum, Recklinghausen: 108

Louvre, Département des Antiquités égyptiennes, Paris: 48/49, 50/51b, 53b, 65, 91b, 96/97, 102

Metropolitan Museum of Art, New York: 26b, 27b, 34, 43, 50/51a, 56

Museo Archeologico, Florence: 76b

Museo Egizio, Turin: 82

Museum of Fine Arts, Boston: 5, 8, 28, 29, 31, 84/85a

Oriental Institute of the University of Chicago: 21

Rijksmuseum van Oudheden, Leiden: 30, 75a, 80a

Sameh, W. E., Cairo: 10, 15a, 17b, 18, 19, 20b, 25, 64, 81, 88b

Seider, R., Heidelberg: 89

Staatliche Museen, Ägyptische Abteilung, Berlin: 4, 36, 37, 45, 47a+b, 52a, 60, 61, 70, 71, 76a, 84/85b, 87, 90, 91a, 93, 98, 99, 103, 104, 107, 109

Staatliche Museen, Frühchristlich-byzantinische Abteilung, Berlin: 112

Staatliche Museen, Münzkabinett, Berlin: 100b

Staatliche Museen, Ägyptische Abteilung, Berlin-Charlottenburg: 2b, 11, 20a, 27a, 57, 59, 62, 67, 74

Staatliche Museen, Antiken-Abteilung, Berlin-Charlottenburg: 106

State Hermitage, Leningrad: 111

State Pushkin Museum of Fine Arts, Moscow: 50/51c, 52b, 110

University College, London: 66

Virginia Museum of Fine Arts, Richmond: 105

Wiesner, H., Bremen: 3

Zentrale Farbbildagentur Düsseldorf: 6

Plates

◄ Figure of a Woman, Brooklyn
▷ Figure of a Woman, Bremen
▽ Woman Standing in a Barrel, Berlin

3

△ Statuette of a Woman Holding a Child, Berlin
▷ Group Statue of King Mycerinus with his
Consort Khamerernebty II, Boston

5

▲ Statues of Princess Nofret and Prince Rahotep, Cairo
▷ Fertility Goddess, Cairo

6

▲ Queen Meresankh III and her Mother Hetepheres II, Gizeh
◄ Group Statue of Queen Meresankh III with her Mother Hetepheres II, Boston

△ Family Group of the Dwarf Seneb, Cairo
▷ Group of the Mortuary Priest Thenti with his Wife, Berlin-Charlottenburg

14

◄ King Pepi II
as a Youth, on the Lap
of his Mother
Ankhnesmeryre,
Brooklyn

△ Women Sifting Corn, Cairo
◁ Maidservant Grinding Grain, Cairo

17

△ Woman Nursing an Infant, Berlin-Charlottenburg
▷ Statuette of a Maidservant, Cairo

20

▲ Semitic Women, Bani Hasan

21

△ Hairdresser Inenu with a Lock of Hair, Brooklyn
▷ King Mentuhotpe II with a Lady of the Harem, Munich

22

23

▲ Head of the Sphinx of an Unknown Princess, Brooklyn

▷ Dressing Scene, Cairo

24

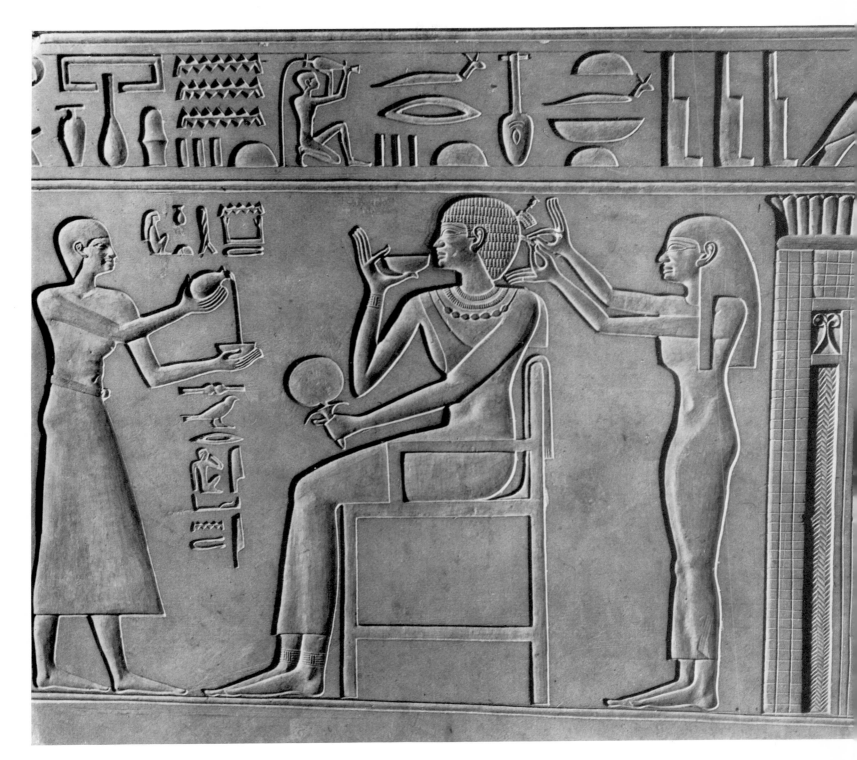

◀ Princess Sebeknakht Nursing Her Child, Brooklyn
▽ Two Women with a Child, New York

26

 Statuette of a Maidservant, Berlin-Charlottenburg
▽ Top of the Statuette of a Woman, New York

△ Head of Princess Sennuwy
◁ Statue of Princess Sennuwy, Boston

29

△ Group of Offering-Bearers, Boston
◁ Statuette of Imeretnebes, Leiden

▲ Woman's Head, Cairo

36

▲ Ladies at a Banquet, Berlin
◄ Nursing Goddess, Berlin

37

◄ Ladies' Orchestra, Thebes
▽ Two Maidservants Decorating a Lady for a Banquet, Thebes

△ Banqueting Party, London

▷ Ladies' Party and Young Female Musicians, London

43

△ Princesses, Berlin
◁ Head of Queen Tiy, Cairo

45

△ Married Couple, Thebes

Two Ointment Flasks, Berlin
▷ Pregnant Woman
▽ Mother and Child

47

Four Offering Utensils in the Shape of Spoons, Paris

49

Three Offering Utensils in the Shape of Swimming Maidens,
New York, Paris, Moscow

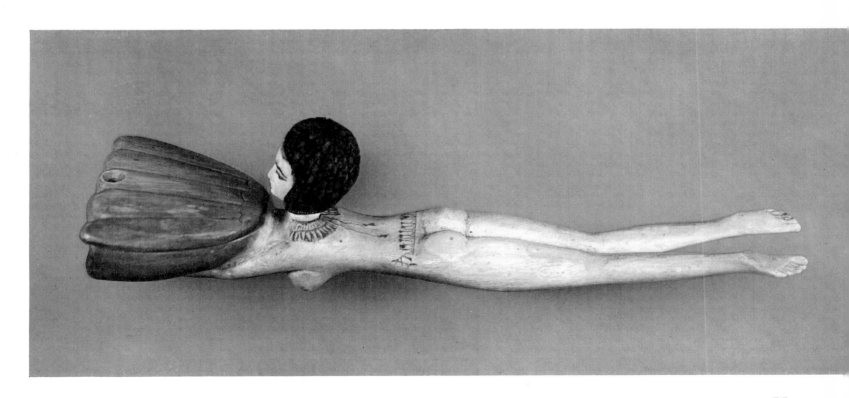

△ Seated Girl, Berlin
▷ Statuette of the Female Singer of Amon Rannai, Moscow

52

Two Statuettes of Women, Paris, Brooklyn

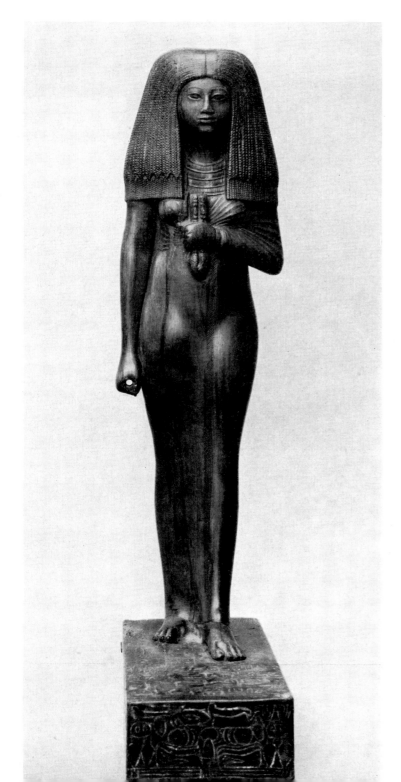

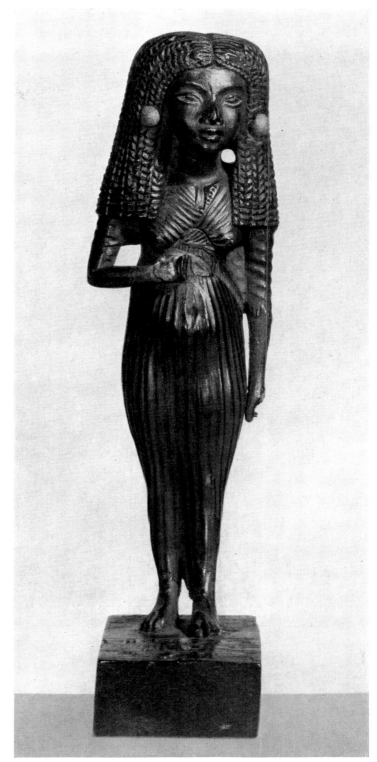

53

54

△ Akhenaten's Family beneath the Radiating Aten, Berlin·Charlottenburg

△ Two Princesses from Tell el Amarna, Oxford
▷ Head of Queen Tiy, Berlin-Charlottenburg

58

60

◄ Head of a Queen of Amarna, Berlin
▼ Statuette of Queen Nefertiti, Berlin

62

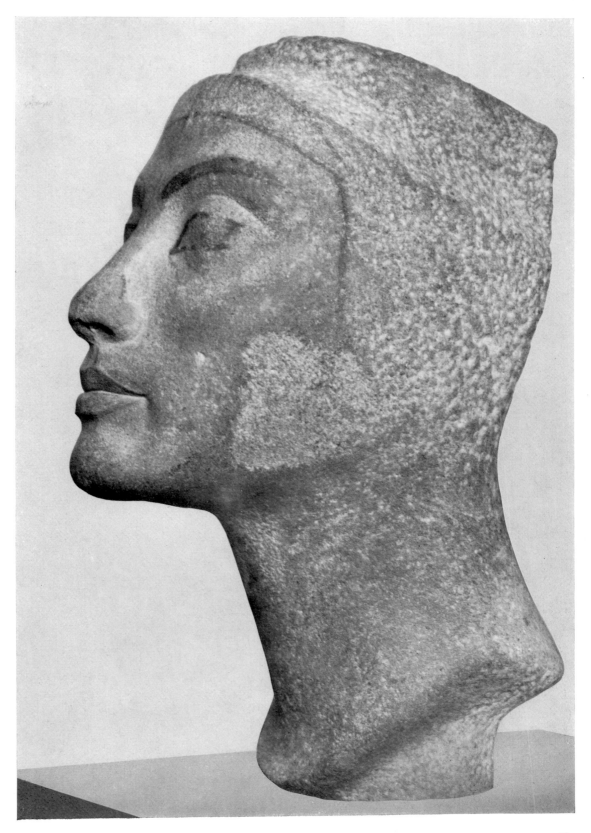

◁ Bust of Queen Nefertiti,
Berlin-Charlottenburg
▷ Head of Queen Nefertiti,
Cairo

64

65

◁ Torso of an Amarna Princess,
London
▷ Promenade in the Garden,
Berlin-Charlottenburg

66

△ ▷ Tutankhamon with His Consort Ankhesenamen

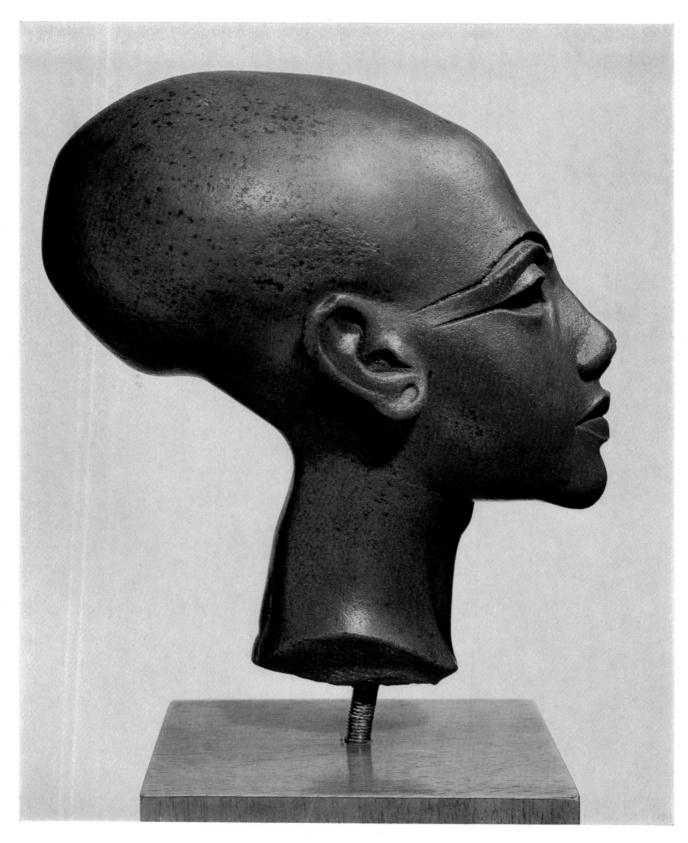

70

△ Stucco Mask of a Woman, Berlin
◁ Head of an Amarna Princess, Berlin

71

△ Women Dancing, Cairo
▷ Detail of the Relief of Dancing Women

72

◄ Married Couple,
Berlin-Charlottenburg

Two Ointment Vessels in the Shape of
Young Maidens, Leiden, Durham

75

△ Face of a Woman, Berlin
▷ Top of the Statuette of a Woman, Florence

76

◁ Statue of Queen Tuy, Mother of
  Ramses II, Rome
▷ Goddess of the West, Thebes

79

▷ Bowl with a Female Lute Player, Leiden
▽ Queen Nefertari Playing a Board Game,
   Thebes

▷ Two Women under
   a Fig Tree, Thebes

△ Female Dancer Turning an Acrobatic Somersault, Turin
▷ Queen Nefertari, Thebes

82

Three Mirror Handles, Boston, Berlin, Brooklyn

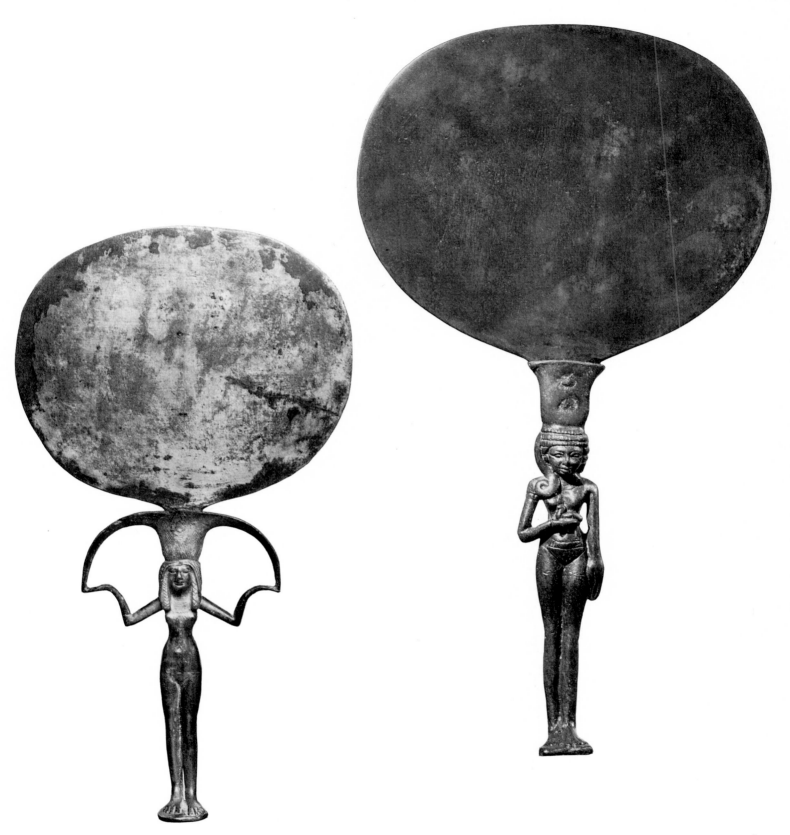

85

◁ Woman Mourning,
Cairo

▶ Top of the Coffin
of Djedmutiues-
ankh, Berlin

◄ Married Couple Drinking Water
from a Garden Pond, Thebes
▶ The Sky Goddess Nut, Heidelberg
▽ Family of Inherkha, Thebes

88

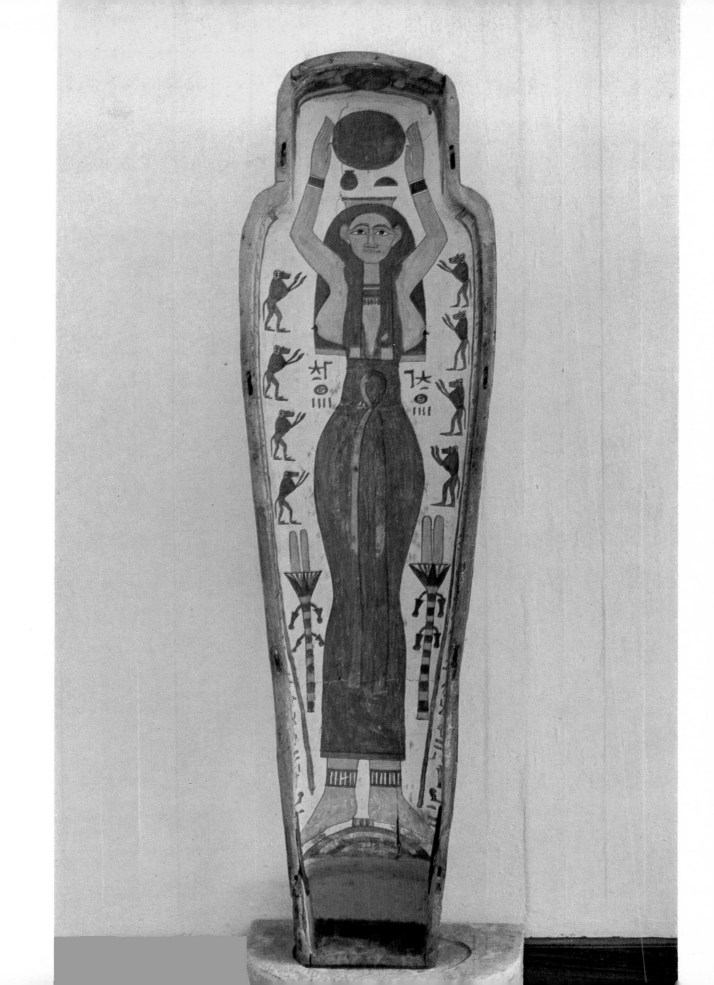

△ Statue of the Divine Consort Karomama, Paris
◄ Statue of a Queen of Ramses II, Berlin

91

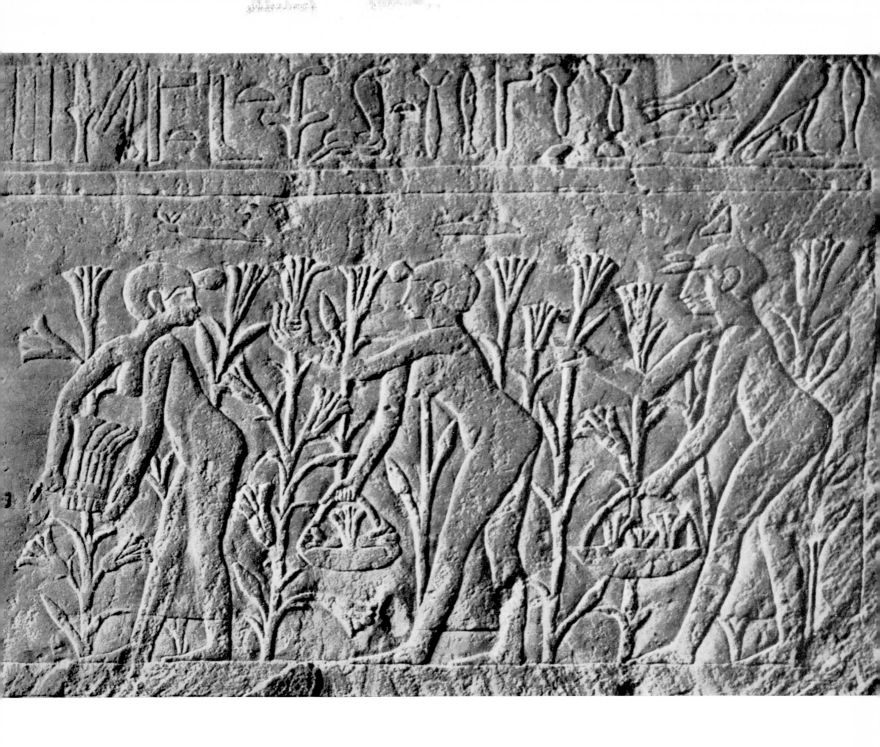

▲ Women Picking and Pressing Lilies to Make Perfume, Paris

98

△ Offering-Bearers, Berlin
◁ Upper Part of a Statue of a Ptolemaic Queen, Berlin

► Mummy Portrait of a Young Girl, Cairo

▲ So-called Cleopatra (VII), London
► Coin Bearing Cleopatra VII's Head, Berlin

104

△ Head of the City Goddess Tyche Wearing the Mural Crown, Moscow
▷ Roundel with the Earth Goddess Ge in the Shape of a Young Woman, Leningrad

110

◄ The Divine Mother Nursing
Her Child
(Maria Lactans),
Berlin